Plant Parts

Name _____

Whether you live in the warm Florida Everglades, t... ...
Columbia, or someplace in between, you live in a world of green, flo...
plants. Look at the plants that grow near you. Can you name the plants' parts?
Green, flowering plants have six basic parts: root, stem, flower, fruit, leaf, and
seed.

Label the parts of the bean plant using the words from the word bank.

Word Bank

flower
fruit
leaf
root
seed
stem

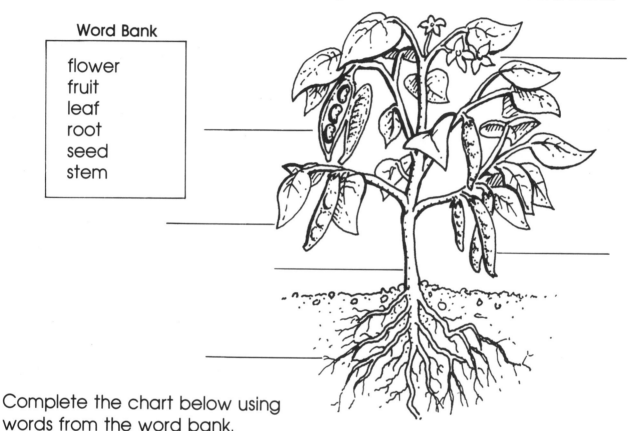

Complete the chart below using words from the word bank.

Plant Part	Function
_____	grows into a new plant
_____	holds and protects the seeds
_____	carries water from the roots to the leaves and food from the leaves to the roots
_____	holds the plant in the soil and collects water and minerals from the soil
_____	makes food for the plant
_____	makes new seeds through reproduction

What's Blooming?

Name _____

Flowers vary greatly in size, color, and shape. The blossoms of grass are so tiny that we rarely see them, while the flower of the chrysanthemum is large and beautiful. But all flowers have basically the same parts and the same important function–to produce seeds.

Look carefully at the picture of the apple blossom. Notice the five parts. The tulip and the lily are very similar. Label the five parts of the lily and the tulip using words from the word bank. Then complete the chart.

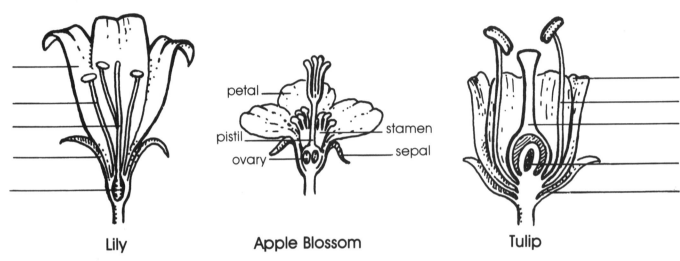

Lily   Apple Blossom   Tulip

Word Bank

ovary
petal
pistil
sepal
stamen

Flower Part	Description
_____	small leaf-like structure at the base of the flower
_____	attractive leaves that are often colorful and sweetly scented
_____	ball-shaped structure where the seeds develop
_____	large center stalk, often shaped like a water bottle
_____	slender stalks with knobbed tips holding grains of pollen

Something Special

Florists usually throw away flowers that are beginning to look wilted and unattractive. Ask a florist for any flowers that are ready to be thrown away. Take the flowers apart and try to identify the parts.

More Flowers

Name _____

Flowers have the important function of producing seeds. The male part of a flower is called the **stamen**. At the tip of the stamen is the **anther**, a tiny case with many grains of **pollen**. The female part of a flower is called the **pistil**. The tip of the pistil is the **stigma**, the long neck is the **style**, and the large base is the **ovary**. The ovary holds the tiny **ovules**, which develop into seeds.

Label the parts of the flower using the words in bold from above.

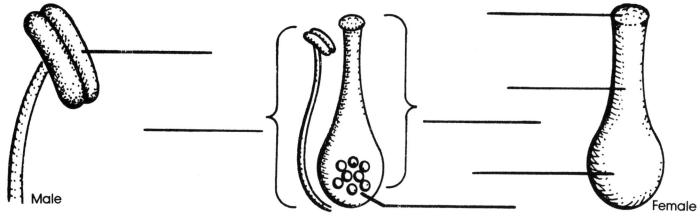

Male   Female

Complete each sentence with the missing word.

1. The anther is filled with ____ ____ ____ ____ ____ ____.
   ₁

2. The stigma is held up by the ____ ____ ____ ____ ____.

3. The female flower part is the ____ ____ ____ ____ ____ ____.
                                          2   6

4. Seeds form in the ____ ____ ____ ____ ____.
                              5

5. Seeds develop from tiny ____ ____ ____ ____ ____ ____.
                                       3

6. The tip of the pistil is the ____ ____ ____ ____ ____ ____.
                                  8   4

7. The male flower part is the ____ ____ ____ ____ ____ ____.
                                              7

Something Special

Use the numbered letters to answer the riddle.

"If April showers bring May flowers, what do May flowers bring?

____ ____ ____ ____ ____ ____ ____ ____
  1   2   3   4   5   6   7   8

Gold Dust

Name _____

Golden grains of pollen are encased in the anther on the top of the stamen. When these golden grains touch the stigma, a long pollen tube grows down to the ovary. The pollen cells meet with the ovule to form a seed. This process is called **fertilization.**

Some flowers have both male and female parts. These plants can fertilize themselves. However, the pollen usually comes from another flower. The pollen grains travel in the wind, by insects, or by birds. Why do you think many fruit growers keep beehives in their orchards?

Study the pictures below. Tell how each flower is being pollinated.

Number the following sentences in the proper order.

_____ Pollen grains fall on the stigma.

_____ Pollen forms on the stamen.

_____ The ovule and pollen form a seed.

_____ A pollen tube grows down to the ovary.

_____ Pollen cells meet with the ovule.

Find Out

Bees store pollen in waxed cells in the hive. This stored pollen, called "bee bread," is used to feed baby bees. How do bees carry pollen?

Anchors Away!

Have you ever tried to pull a large plant out of the ground? Sometimes it can be quite a struggle. That's because roots are holding it in place.

Roots do more than hold a plant in the ground. They also collect water and minerals for the plant.

There are two kinds of root systems. Some plants have shallow roots with many branches. These are called **fibrous roots.** The other root system has only one main root that digs deep into the ground. This is called the **tap root.**

Water gathering is not done by large, thick roots; thick roots have a waterproof, outside layer. Instead, hundreds of small, fine roots, called **root hairs,** have the job of collecting water and minerals.

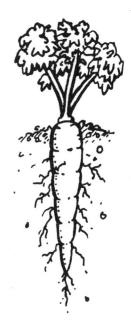

_____   _____

Label the type of root system. Also label the root hairs.

It has been a long, dry, hot summer. Mr. Williams' grass is turning brown, but the dandelions are bright green.

1. What kind of root system does his grass have? _____

2. What kind of root system do his dandelions have? _____

3. Why does the dandelion stay green while the grass turns brown? _____

_____

4. Draw the root systems for the grass and dandelions.

Fun Facts

The tap root of an alfalfa plant can grow as much as four meters deep in one season!

 IF8759 Science Enrichment

Food Factories

Name _____

Leaves are like little factories designed to do an important job–make food. Different parts of the leaf help with this job. The **veins** in a leaf are bundles of tiny tubes. They carry water and minerals to the leaf and take food from the leaf to the rest of the plant. Veins also help hold the leaf up.

On the underside of the leaf are small openings called **stomata.** Stomata have been called the lungs of a leaf because they allow **air** to enter the leaf.

The outer layers of the leaf are covered with a **waxy** layer which prevents the leaf from drying out.

Why are leaves green? Leaf cells contain small particles called chloroplasts. Each chloroplast contains a complex, green material called **chlorophyll** which gives the leaf its color.

Label the parts of the leaf using words from the word bank.

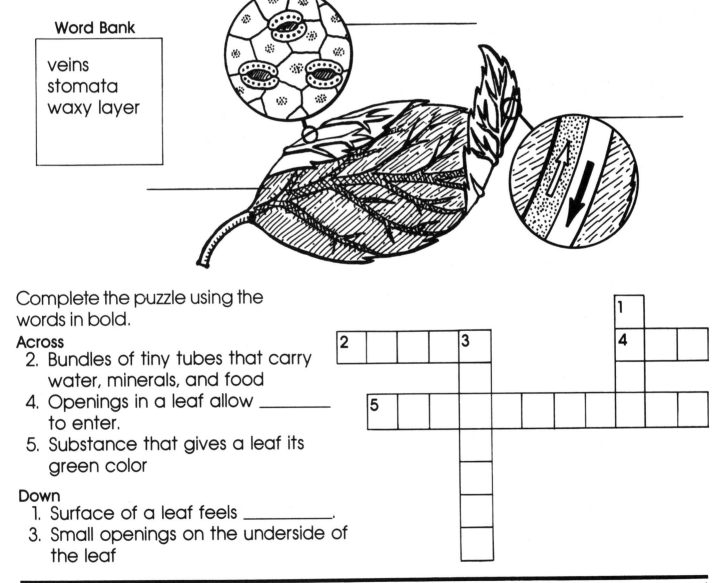

Word Bank

veins
stomata
waxy layer

Complete the puzzle using the words in bold.

Across
2. Bundles of tiny tubes that carry water, minerals, and food
4. Openings in a leaf allow _____ to enter.
5. Substance that gives a leaf its green color

Down
1. Surface of a leaf feels _____.
3. Small openings on the underside of the leaf

Food from the Sun

Name _____

With the help of chlorophyll and energy from the sun, a leaf can change lifeless substances into food. This process is called **photosynthesis.**

Plants need **water (H₂O)** and **carbon dioxide (CO₂)** to make food by photosynthesis. The water is gathered by the plant's roots. Carbon dioxide, found in the air, is gathered through tiny openings, called stomata, located on the underside of the leaf.

The leaf uses **chlorophyll** and **sunlight** to change water and carbon dioxide into oxygen and sugar. The sugar is mixed with water and sent to other parts of the plant. Oxygen is released into the air through the stomata.

Complete the formula for photosynthesis using the words in bold above.

Photosynthesis = _____ + _____ + _____ + _____

Scott's dad gave him some healthy houseplants. Scott decided to keep them in his room, but his room was always dark. What do you think will happen to Scott's plants? Why?

_____

_____

_____

Sarah set up her aquarium with some fish and aquatic plants. Explain how the fish and the plants benefit from each other.

_____

_____

_____

Find Out

To make one-half kg of sugar, a plant must breathe over one million liters of air. What kind of plants produce the sugar that is in the sugar bowl in your kitchen?

Plant Pipelines

How does the plant get its food? Thin tubes in the stem carry food from the leaf to the rest of the plant. Other tubes carry water and minerals from the roots to the leaves. Both kinds of tubes are found in bundles in the stem.

The tube bundles are arranged in two ways. A **monocot** stem has bundles scattered throughout the stem. **Dicot** stems have their bundles arranged in a ring around the edge of the stem.

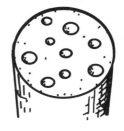 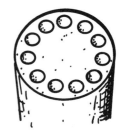

_____ _____

Dicot or monocot stem? Label the two pictures above.

Experiment: Observing Plant Pipelines

Materials:
- drinking glass
- water
- food coloring
- eye dropper
- knife
- stalk of celery

Directions:
Put a few drops of food coloring in a glass of water. Trim off the bottom 2 cm of a stalk of celery. Place the celery in the water. Let stand for 3-4 hours.

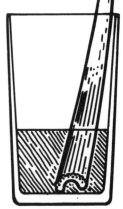

Results:

1. Describe what you see. _____

_____

2. Cut the stalk crosswise. Look at the cut ends. What do you see?

_____

3. What carried the water up the stalk? _____

4. What would happen if the stem of a plant were broken? Why?

_____

Something Special

Try the experiment above, but with a new twist. Use a white flower instead of celery; carnations or daisies work great. Watch what happens!

Cone-Bearing Plants

Name _____

Plants, like pine trees, that develop seeds in cones are called **conifers.**
Conifers have two kinds of cones. The smaller male cone develops pollen grains.
Egg cells develop in the ovule of the much larger female cone. Pollen from the
male cone is carried by the wind and lodges in the scales of the female cone. A
pollen tube grows down to the ovule, and a new seed is formed. After the seeds
are ripe, the cone and the seed drop to the ground.

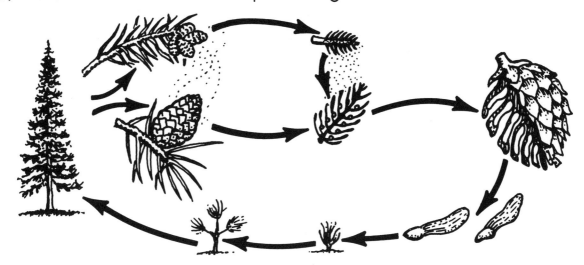

1. In what way is seed formation in a conifer the same as in a flowering plant? _____

_____

2. How is seed formation in a conifer different than in a flowering plant?_____

_____

Number the following steps in the correct order.

_____ A seed is formed.

_____ A new conifer sprouts from the seed.

_____ Pollen grains are carried by the wind.

_____ A pollen tube grows down to the ovule.

_____ Pollen grains lodge in the scales of the female cone.

_____ Ripened seeds are released from the cone.

Fun Facts

The giant redwood trees are unquestionably the world's tallest trees. The
largest of these conifers, found in Humboldt County, California, has been
measured at over 100 meters tall.

Fiddleheads to Ferns

Name _____

Have you ever seen little green "fiddleheads" growing out of the moist soil? These will soon be beautiful **ferns.** Ferns, like flowering green plants, have roots, stems, and leaves. But they do not make seeds. Ferns reproduce from **spores.** Most ferns are about 25 cm tall, but some are as small as 2 cm or as tall as trees!

Tiny brown dots, containing hundreds of spores, line the underside of the fern leaf. Spores that fall on a wet place grow into tiny heart-shaped plants. Each tiny plant produces both the sperm and the egg cells. After a rain, the sperm cell will swim to the egg cell through the water. When the sperm fertilizes an egg cell, a new young fern will grow. Making food by photosynthesis, the young fiddlehead will grow into a mature fern plant.

Complete the chart using information from above.

Plant parts	
How the fern makes food	
Size of plant	
Method of reproducing	

1. Why must ferns live in wet places? _____

_____

2. How are ferns like flowering plants? _____

_____

3. How are ferns different than flowering plants? _____

_____

Find Out

Millions of years ago, the earth was covered with ferns. Today, there is still evidence of these giant plants. The products of these plants are extremely valuable to man. Can you name the products? How were they formed?

Nature's Green Carpet

Name _____

Have you ever seen a smooth, green, velvety carpet growing on a moist forest floor? This carpet is made of hundreds of tiny **moss** plants growing closely together.

Mosses, like ferns, do not produce seeds; they reproduce with spores. Sperm cells and egg cells are formed at the top of the moss plant. After a rain, the sperm travels through the water to the egg cell. The fertilized egg cell sprouts a tall stalk with a case for the spores at its tip. These spores will produce new mosses. Mosses make their food by photosynthesis, but unlike other green plants, they do not have roots, leaves, or stems. Mosses are small and grow only a few centimeters high. Food and water travel slowly from cell to cell.

Complete the chart using the information from above.

Plant parts	
How it gets its food	
Size	
Method of reproducing	

1. Why must mosses live in wet places? _____

_____

2. How are mosses like ferns? _____

_____

3. How are mosses different from other green plants? _____

_____

Find Out

An old woodsman's survival tip says, "Moss usually grows on the north side of a tree." Why is this usually true?

Fungus Among Us

Name _____

"Yuch! This bread has green fuzz on it!!" The fuzz is mold. Mold and mushrooms are **fungi.**

A fungus plant is not a true plant, because it does not have roots, **stems, leaves,** or **chlorophyll.** Fungi cannot make their own **food** like green plants. Instead, they get their energy by absorbing food from dead or living matter.

Most fungi reproduce by forming **spores.** The spores fall on dead organisms. A tiny cell breaks out of the spore and grows into fuzzy threads. The threads form new caps, stalks, or capsules.

Fungi are helpful members of nature's recycling team. They help break down dead organisms that can then become part of the **soil.**

Complete the following sentences using the words in bold.

1. Most fungi reproduce by forming __ __ __ __ __ __.
                                     7

2. Fungi do not have roots, __ __ __ __ __, or __ __ __ __ __ __.
                              1 3

3. Fungi cannot make their own __ __ __ __.
                                 6

4. Fungi are not green; they lack __ __ __ __ __ __ __ __ __ __ __.
                                    5   4

5. Mold and mushrooms are __ __ __ __ __.
                           2

6. Fungi break down dead organisms that then become part

   of the __ __ __ __.

Use the numbered letters to solve the riddle.

"What kind of room has no walls, windows, or doors?"

__ __ __ __ __ __ __ __
1 2 3 4 5 6 7 1

Find Out

Get an unwashed mushroom from a store. Cut off the mushroom cap. Place the cap, gill side down, on a sheet of paper. Place a bowl over the cap. Let it set for one day. Remove the bowl and mushroom cap. Presto! It's a print. What is that dust that formed the print?

Baker's Buddy

Name _____

   Yeast is another kind of fungus. Yeast differs from other fungi in two ways. First, yeast is made of only one cell. Second, yeast can reproduce in two ways. Each cell can grow a small bump, called a **bud.** When this bud grows large enough, it breaks off and forms a new cell. This is called **budding.** The second way of reproducing is when the cell divides two or three times inside the cell case. The new cells become spores and stay inside until the case breaks open.

   Yeast grows rapidly when it has sugar for food. When yeast breaks down the sugar, it gives off carbon dioxide gas bubbles and alcohol. These bubbles cause bread dough to swell up. Yeast really is a baker's buddy!

Answer the following questions by unscrambling the letters in each yeast cell. The letters will "bud" into the correct answers.

1. Yeast is a kind of _____.

2. Yeast is made of only one _____.

3. Reproducing by making little bumps is

    called _____.

4. Yeast divides in the cell case and forms

    _____.

5. Yeast feeds on _____.

6. Yeast produces bubbles of _____.

Find Out

Find out what Matza is. How does it get its name?

Algae

Name _____

Algae can be found growing on the sides of your aquarium, in puddles in your yard, as seaweed in the ocean, or almost any place where there is water.

Algae is one of the simplest forms of plant life. Like fungus, algae does not have roots, stems, or leaves. Unlike fungus, algae has chlorophyll and can make its own food by photosynthesis.

Algae can range in size from single cells to the giant Pacific kelp that grows to a length of sixty centimeters!

1. In what ways is algae similar to fungi? _____

_____

2. In what way is algae different than fungi? _____

_____

	Complete the chart using the information from above.
	Size
	How it makes food
	Habitat
	Plant parts

Find Out

Lichens are some of the plant world's most unusual organisms. Actually, lichens are two organisms–algae and fungi–that live together. Do some research on lichens. Why are lichens so unusual? Could algae and fungi survive alone? Explain.

A World of Plants

Name _____

From the small, one-celled algae to the giant redwood trees, our world is filled with thousands of different kinds of plants. Scientists have a special way of classifying, or grouping, the many kinds of plants. Study the diagram below.

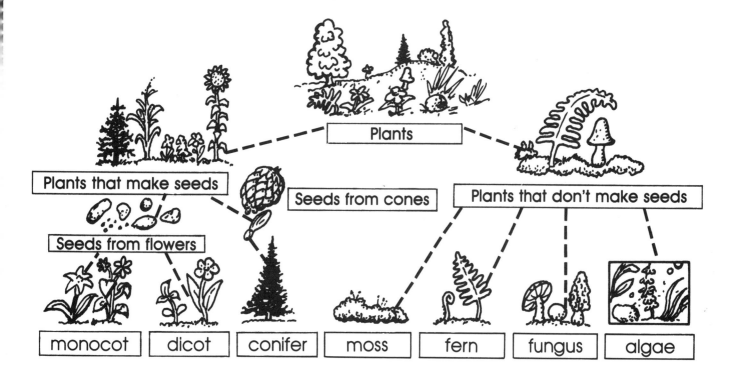

Look carefully at the plant characteristics listed below. Place a (✔) in the column or columns that represent the plant with that characteristic.

	monocot	dicot	conifer	moss	fern	fungus	algae
1. is green							
2. makes seeds							
3. makes seeds in a flower							
4. flower made seed with two seed parts							
5. flower made seed with one seed part							
6. makes seeds in a cone							
7. produces spores							
8. has leaves with veins							
9. has leaves with parallel veins							
10. has leaves with net-like veins							
11. has needle-like leaves							
12. one-celled plant							

IF8759 Science Enrichment

Puzzling Plants

Name _____

Complete the puzzle using the words from the word bank.

Across
1. Gold dust found in the stamen
3. Makes seeds in a cone
4. Product of photosynthesis
7. Means of reproduction for ferns, molds, and yeast
8. See diagram.
11. Plant's food making process
12. See diagram.

Down
1. See diagram.
2. See diagram.
3. Green coloring in leaves
5. See diagram.
6. See diagram.
7. See diagram.
9. See diagram.
10. Two food parts.

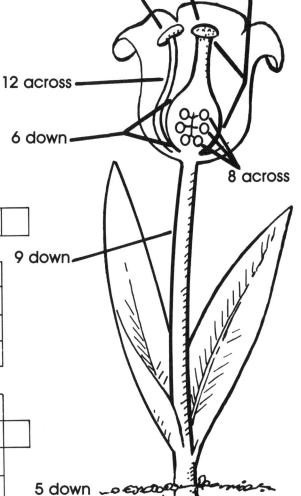

Word Bank

anther	ovary	pollen	stem
chlorophyll	ovules	root	stigma
conifer	photosynthesis	spores	sugar
dicot	pistil	stamen	

Classy Creatures

Name _____

___ ___ ___ ___ ___ ___ ___ ___

Scientists use a special tool to help them find the names of insects, trees, and many other things. It is called a **dichotomist key.**

Each of the creatures above has a name. We will use our own dichotomist key to give each creature its name. To use the key, work with only one creature at a time. First read steps 1a and 1b. Decide which statement is true about the creature. Then follow the directions after that step. The directions will lead you to a new pair of steps. Keep this up until you come to a step that gives you the creature's name. Write the creature's name in the space provided. After you have named all of the creatures, you will be able to complete the following sentence.

A dichotomist key is used to ___ ___ ___ ___ ___ ___ ___ ___.

If this is true,   **do this.**

1 a.	The creature has two eyes.	Go to step 2.
b.	The creature has one eye.	Go to step 5.
2 a.	The creature has one or more antennae.	Go to step 3.
b.	The creature has no antennae.	Its name is "L."
3 a.	The creature has one antenna.	Its name is "I."
b.	The creature has more than one antenna.	Go to step 4.
4 a.	The creature has two antennae.	Its name is "S."
b.	The creature has three antennae.	Its name is "Y."
5 a.	The creature has one or more antennae.	Go to step 6.
b.	The creature has no antennae.	Its name is "A."
6 a.	The creature has one antenna.	Its name is "F."
b.	The creature has two antennae.	Its name is "C."

Something Special

Draw your own friendly creature from space. Give your creature from zero to three antennae and one or two eyes. Have a friend use the dichotomist key above to find what letter the creature is wearing.

Backbone or No Backbone

Name _____

The animal kingdom can be divided into two groups, **vertebrates** and **invertebrates.** Vertebrates are animals with backbones. The backbone is made of several bones called **vertebrae.** Each vertabra is separated by a thin disc of cartilage. The backbone supports the body and helps the animal move.

Invertebrates are animals without backbones. Have you ever looked closely at an ant or fly? They do not have a backbone or any other bones in their bodies. Some invertebrates, like crabs and lobsters, have hard, outer-body coverings. Some invertebrates, like worms, are soft all the way through their bodies.

Circle all of the hidden animals in the puzzle below. Then list them in their own group.

Word Bank

butterfly	skunk
cow	snail
crayfish	snake
deer	spider
dog	swan
fish	wasp
grasshopper	worm

```
N J W O R M E Z R A C D
G R A S S H O P P E R E
F K B P D S W A N P A E
S N A I L Q W C S X Y R
K E V D O G A I N C F G
U P S E A J S S A O I X
N O L R W M P H K F S C
K T F I S H G B E Y H O
U B U T T E R F L Y T W
```

Vertebrates

_____

_____

_____

_____

_____

_____

Invertebrates

_____

_____

_____

_____

_____

_____

Find Out

About 1,000,000 kinds of animals have been classified by scientists. Only 45,000 are vertebrates. How many are invertebrates?

Warm and Cold-Blooded Animals

Name _____

Mammals and birds are **warm-blooded** animals. Warm-blooded animals maintain a constant body temperature with the help of hair or feathers as insulation. Warm-blooded animals are called **endothermic** animals.

Cold-blooded animals, such as fish, reptiles, and amphibians, get their body heat from their surroundings. Their body temperature varies according to the temperature of their environment. Cold-blooded animals are called **ectothermic** animals.

Circle all of the animals in the wordsearch below using the words from the word bank. Then list the animals in the proper group.

Word Bank

bear	rat
deer	salamander
duck	shark
eagle	snake
fox	toad
frog	trout
lizard	turtle
owl	

```
I  E  K  M  O  W  L  D  B  U
S  A  L  A  M  A  N  D  E  R
T  G  I  A  S  L  T  O  A  D
U  L  Z  F  H  D  E  E  R  S
R  E  A  R  A  U  O  E  G  N
T  R  R  O  R  C  F  O  X  A
L  A  D  G  K  K  P  F  N  K
E  T  R  O  U  T  B  R  M  E
```

Warm-Blooded

Mammal	Bird

Cold-Blooded

Fish	Reptile	Amphibian

Find Out

Mammals cool off by sweating. Horses sweat through their skin, and coyotes sweat through their tongues when panting. How do your family pets cool off? How do they stay warm?

Survival

An adult frog lays hundreds of eggs at one time. You would think that most ponds would be overrun with frogs. Many of these eggs will hatch, but very few offspring will survive. Most will be eaten by larger animals. Only the fittest survive. The fittest are those that **adapt** to their environment.

What does **adapt** mean? _____

_____

_____

What adaptions help each of these animals survive?

deer _____

mouse _____

skunk _____

rabbit _____

turtle _____

porcupine _____

Something Special

Create an animal of your own. Give your animal some special defense adaptions.

animal's name _____   enemies _____

habitat _____   defenses _____

food _____   _____

Best Foot Forward

Name _____

Like other animals, birds have adaptions that help them survive. A duck would not swim well if it had the feet of a robin. A woodpecker would not find too many insects if it had the bill of a duck. Can you imagine an owl trying to grab a mouse if it had feet like a duck?

Examine each of the different types of bills and feet pictured below. Match each with one of the advantages listed below. Then use another source to help find a bird that has each feature.

 Bird _____
Advantage_____
_____

 Bird _____
Advantage_____
_____

 Bird _____
Advantage_____
_____

Bird _____
Advantage_____
_____

 Bird _____
Advantage_____
_____

 Bird _____
Advantage_____
_____

 Bird _____
Advantage_____
_____

 Bird _____
Advantage_____
_____

Advantages (bills)

cracking seeds
straining water for food
tearing flesh
probing for insects

Advantages (feet)

climbing trees
swimming
grabbing onto animals
perching

Something Special

Create your own unique bird. Write a paragraph that describes your bird's habitat, food, enemies, and size. Give your bird a name. Draw a picture of it.

Invertebrates

Name _____

Just three groups of the many kinds of invertebrates are listed below. The first group are **arthropods.** Arthropods are invertebrates with jointed legs. Insects, spiders, and crustaceans, like lobsters and crabs, belong to this group. **Worms** are slender, creeping animals with soft bodies and no legs. The last group are **mollusks.** Mollusks are also soft-bodied, but most have shells for protection. Some mollusks, like the octopus, do not have shells.

Using the words from the word bank, find some examples of invertebrates in the puzzle below. Then list them under the group they belong to.

```
M F T A P E W O R M F
C R A Y F I S H O S L
L O B S T E R D U O A
A P L Q C M C H N C T
M T I U W O R A D T W
S N A I L T A J W O O
S K N D B H B E O P R
A N T O Y S T E R U M
E A R T H W O R M S O
```

Word Bank

ant	crayfish	lobster	oyster	squid
clam	earthworm	moth	roundworm	tapeworm
crab	flatworm	octopus	snail	

Arthropods	Worms	Mollusks
_____	_____	_____
_____	_____	_____
_____	_____	_____
_____	_____	_____
_____	_____	_____

Fun Fact

The longest known species of giant earthworm is found in South Africa and is 136 cm long!

Animals with a Double Life

Name _____

Amphibians are cold-blooded vertebrates. The word **amphibia** means to live a double life. Some amphibians live exclusively on land or in the water, while others live in both habitats. Frogs, toads, and salamanders are three of the most common amphibians.

Adult frogs and toads are able to hear you sneak up on them because they have large eardrums, called **tympanums.** Salamanders do not have eardrums but sense vibrations through their legs.

Frogs and toads develop from eggs that are laid in the water. The larval forms of the frog and toad are called **tadpoles.** Salamanders hatch from eggs within the adult.

Use the pictures and information above to complete the chart. Make a (✓) in the correct box or boxes.

	Frog	Toad	Salamander
smooth skin			
bumpy skin			
nostrils			
tympanum			
tail			
strong hind legs			
backbone			
warm-blooded			
cold-blooded			

Find Out

Egg-Tadpole-Frog. These are the three stages of a frog's life cycle. What adaptions help the frog get food? What adaptions help the frog breathe in each stage? What adaptions give the frog movement in each stage?

Food Chains

Name _____

What did you have for dinner last night? Perhaps it was chicken. A few days ago that chicken was probably eating corn. You eat chicken, the chicken eats the corn, and the corn grows in the sunshine. This is what we call a **food chain.**

Organisms that make their own food are called **producers.** Corn is a producer. Green plants are producers because they get their energy from the sun. Organisms that do not make their own food are called **consumers.**

Name an important food for each animal pictured below. If that food is also an animal, list an important food for that animal. Keep doing this until you run out of animals.

_____   _____   _____   _____   _____

_____   _____   _____   _____   _____

_____   _____   _____   _____   _____

_____   _____   _____   _____   _____

Which organism starts the food chain below? Place a **1** on that line. Number the rest of the food chain in order. Then place a (✓) in front of all the consumers. Place a (★) in front of the producers.

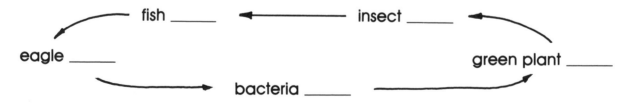

fish _____   insect _____   green plant _____

eagle _____

bacteria _____

Something Special

Try to make a food chain with more than four links. What is the longest food chain you can make?

More Food Chains

Name _____

In the woodland and aquatic communities, there are a large number of food chains. Study the picture on this page.

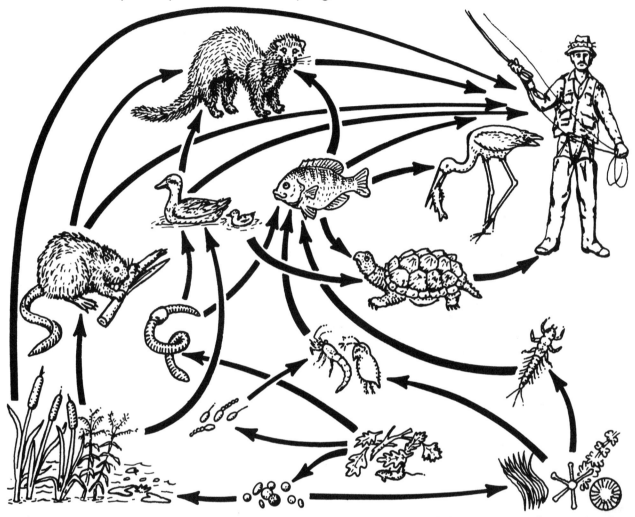

Find at least three food chains in the scene above. List the food chains below.

Food Chain #1	Food Chain #2	Food Chain #3
_____	_____	_____
_____	_____	_____
_____	_____	_____
_____	_____	_____
_____	_____	_____

Find Out

The use of DDT, a chemical insecticide, has been made illegal in many areas. What effect did this poison have on the eagle? How did this affect the eagle population?

Meat, Salad, and Casseroles

Name _____

Animals and plants often get their food from different sources. Plants that make their food from sunlight, air, and water are called **producers.** Animals are **consumers;** they get their food from other sources. Animals that eat only plants are called **herbivores. Carnivores** are animals that eat only meat. **Omnivores** are animals that eat both plants and meat. Which of these are you?

Study the picture below. Then list all the carnivores, herbivores, omnivores, and producers that you can find.

Carnivore	Herbivore	Omnivore	Producer
_____	_____	_____	_____
_____	_____	_____	_____
_____	_____	_____	_____
_____	_____	_____	_____

Something Special

Make a food chain using the organisms found in the picture above. Label each member by writing **C, H, O,** or **P** over each carnivore, herbivore, omnivore, and producer in the chain.

Food Webs

Eating would be boring if we ate only one kind of food. Imagine eating oatmeal for breakfast, lunch, and dinner, 365 days a year, for the rest of your life. Most animals, like humans, eat more than one kind of food. This means that most animals are members of more than one food chain. Separate food chains that interlock are called **food webs.**

Form a food web by drawing arrows from each prey to its predator. Remember–most prey have more than one predator. (Hint: Use a different colored crayon for each food chain.)

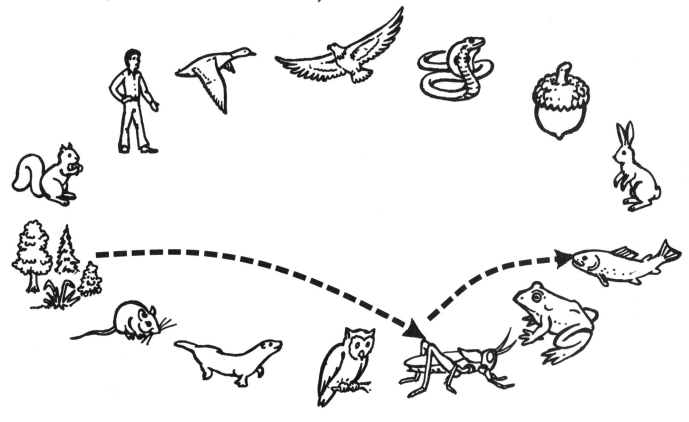

One food chain that you may have found in the food web is this one:

plant ⟶ grasshopper ⟶ trout ⟶ otter

Write two more food chains that you found in your food web.

1._____

_____

2._____

_____

Gone for the Winter

Name _____

When the cold winds blow, some animals travel to other regions for the winter. In the spring, they travel back to their summer habitat. This movement is called **migration.** Some animals migrate to warmer climates to find food. Others, like salmon and whales, migrate to give birth to their young.

Below are three pictures of migration. Choose one of the pictures and write a brief news article for the outdoor section of your newspaper. Good reporters will use the five W's (who, what, where, when, and why) in their articles.

_____

_____

_____

_____

_____

_____

_____

_____

_____

_____

Fun Fact

The monarch butterfly flies south for the winter. Many travel from Ontario, Canada to southern Texas—a distance of over 2,400 km.

A Winter Snooze

Name _____

When winter arrives, some animals enter a sleep called **hibernation.** Most hibernators are **cold**-blooded animals, like snakes, spiders, toads, frogs, and **turtles.** During hibernation, the animal's **heartbeat** and breathing slows down to a point where they are hardly noticeable. Body **temperature** also drops.

Some warm-blooded animals, like bears, raccoons, **chipmunks,** and groundhogs also hibernate. Bears and raccoons do not sleep soundly. They are easily awakened when hibernating. During hibernation, these animals get **energy** from fat that they have stored during the late **summer.**

Finish the crossword puzzle below using the clues and the words in bold for help.

Across
2. Most hibernators are _____ – blooded animals.
4. Body _____ drops during hibernation.
6. The _____ beat slows during hibernation.

Down
1. Shelled reptile that hibernates in muddy pond bottoms
2. Small animal that hibernates in underground burrows
3. The time when animals store fat for the winter
5. Bears get their _____ from stored fat.

Find Out

Which animals stay in the Arctic during the winter? Which animals migrate from the Arctic?

Endangered

Name _____

The only place you will ever see a dodo, a passenger pigeon, or a dinosaur is in a book. These animals no longer live on earth. They are **extinct.** Today, thousands of animals are in danger of becoming extinct.

The jaguar, polar bear, sperm whale, and African elephant are only a few of the many animals that man is responsible for **endangering.** These animals are hunted for meat, fur, and trophies.

Some animals are endangered because their habitats are being destroyed by land development. The green sea turtle is endangered because buildings and crowded beaches now take the place of their nesting grounds.

Most recently, man has polluted the environment with pesticides and fertilizers that have poisoned the food of many animals. Insecticides have entered the bald eagle's food chain, causing the eggs to become thin-shelled and break before hatching.

Use another source to find out the names of some other animals that are endangered or extinct. Then fill in the chart below.

Animal	Endangered or Extinct	Why?
_____	_____	_____
_____	_____	_____
_____	_____	_____
_____	_____	_____
_____	_____	_____

Something Special

Write an editorial for your local newspaper. State your concern for endangered animals and suggest ways that people could help protect these animals.

The Tortoise and the Hare

Name _____

"On your mark. Get set. Go!" The race is on between the tortoise and the hare. Hare speeds away from the starting line at 56 km per hour. Tortoise plods along at less than 1 km per hour.

Many animals depend on their speed to escape from predators. Other animals use their speed to capture their prey. These are the speeds that some animals can travel. Graph the speeds of these animals on the chart below from slowest to fastest. Then answer the questions below.

Animal	Speed (km per hour)
butterfly	19
elephant	40
coyote	72
cheetah	113
grizzly bear	48
housefly	8
salmon	48
sailfish	96
jack rabbit	64
lion	80
human (jogging)	11

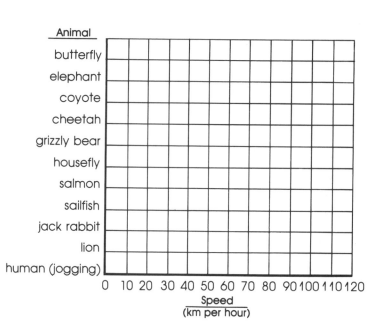

Both the coyote and the rabbit are very fast animals, but each uses its speed in a different way. How does each animal use its speed?

_____

_____

The tortoise is not very fast, but it has other adaptions to aid in protection. How does the tortoise protect itself?

_____

_____

Fun Fact

The Olympic athlete can run 43 km per hour, but only for a very short distance and period of time.

Animal Facts

Name _____

Finish the puzzle below using the words from the word bank.

Word Bank

arthropods
birds
chain
cold
consumers
hair
herbivore
insects
migration
omnivores
producers
scales
spiders
warm
web

Across
1. A series of animals that feed on each other is a food ____.
4. Invertebrates with jointed legs
7. Largest group of invertebrates
9. Reptiles are ____-blooded.
11. Feathered, warm-blooded vertebrates
12. Body covering of mammals
13. Interlocking food chains form a food ____.
15. Organisms that eat both plants and animals

Down
2. Animal that eats only plants
3. Organisms that make their own food
5. Organisms that do not make their own food
6. Seasonal movement of animals
8. Arthropods with eight legs, two body sections, and no antennae
10. Body covering of reptiles
14. Birds and mammals are ____-blooded animals.

"Dem Bones, Dem Dry Bones"

Name _____

Use your science book or another source to help.

Label the skeletal system with the scientific name for each bone.

Matching: Place the letter of the scientific name in the space provided next to the common name.

Common Names
____ skull
____ jawbone
____ collarbone
____ shoulder blade
____ tailbone
____ backbones
____ kneecap
____ thigh bone
____ rib
____ hip bone
____ shin bone
____ lower arm bone

Scientific Names
a. pelvis
b. vertebrae
c. scapula
d. cranium
e. radius
 f. femur
g. mandible
h. tibia
 i. patella
 j. clavicle
k. coccyx
 l. rib

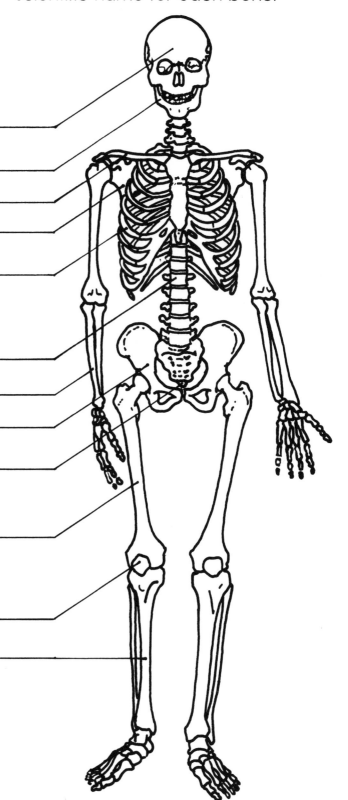

Find Out

When you were born, you had 300 bones in your body. By the time you are an adult, your bones will number 206. Why is this so?

Muscle Power

Name _____

Use your science book or another source to help.

Fill in the blanks with words from the word bank.

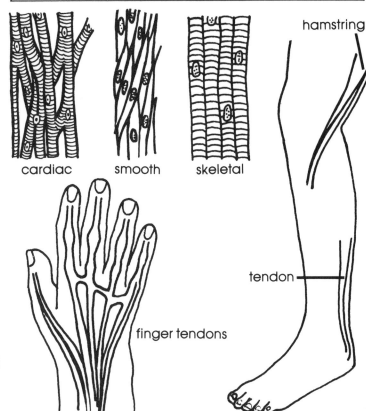

cardiac   smooth   skeletal

hamstring

tendon

finger tendons

There are _____ kinds of muscles. Internal organs, such as the intestines, the stomach, and the esophagus are moved by the _____ muscles. The _____ muscles move your skeleton and external body parts. The heart beat is controlled by the _____ muscle. Muscles which need a special message from your brain in order to work are called _____ muscles. Muscles which move automatically, without conscious thought, are called _____ muscles. The tough cords that connect the skeletal muscles to your bones are called _____.

Fill in the chart.

Activity	Do I need conscious thought to do it?	Voluntary or Involuntary Action	Kind of Muscle
jumping rope			
heart beating			
waving			
breathing			
swallowing food			
pumping blood			
whistling			
running			
digestion			

Find Out

Who is your Achilles' tendon named for and why?

Message Transmissions

Name _____

Use your science book or another source to help. Fill in the spaces with words from the word bank.

Your body has its own system for sending messages to your brain. This system of individual nerves and their pathways is found throughout the body. It is called the **peripheral nervous system.** The peripheral nervous system is a pathway to the brain for your five senses. It also serves your internal organs and helps you respond to your environment.

Messages are sent to the brain through a network of nerve cells called _____. Neurons have long arms, called _____, and shorter arms, called _____.

In order for messages to travel along the pathway, the neurons must connect with each other. This connection is called a _____. Messages enter each neuron through the dendrite. Messages exit the neuron through the axon.

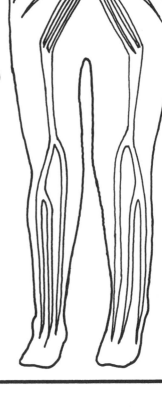

Word Bank

axons
dendrites
synapse
neurons

Color the parts of the nervous system.

brain - gray
spinal cord - blue
nerves - red

Color the parts of the neuron.

nucleus - green
axon - orange
dendrite - purple

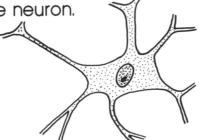

Fun Fact

Sensory nerves send 100 million messages to the brain every second.

Think Fast

Name _____

While riding your bike down the street, a car suddenly pulls out in front of you. Your eyes send a message to your brain. Your brain sends a message to your muscles to apply the brakes. How long did it take you to stop? This time is called your **reaction time.**

Here is a simple experiment to find out your reaction time. The only materials you will need are a 30 cm ruler and a partner.

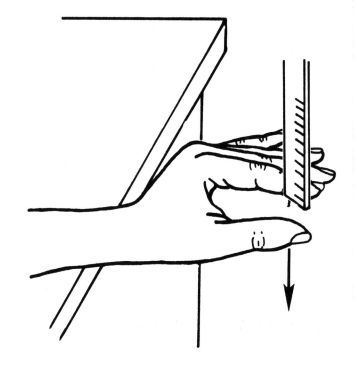

1. Place your left arm on your desk with your hand over the edge.
2. Space your thumb and index finger apart a little more than the thickness of the ruler.
3. Your partner will hold one end of the ruler with the other end level with the top of your index finger.
4. Your partner will say "ready," pause a few seconds, and drop the ruler.
5. Catch the ruler and check the distance by reading the level at the bottom of the index finger.
6. Record your results.
7. Now, try the experiment again with your right hand.

Trial	Left hand	Right hand
1		
2		
3		
4		
5		

Average: _____ _____

Which hand had the fastest reaction time? _____

Fun Fact

Nerve impulses, or messages, travel at 100 meters per second!

Interbody Highway System

Name _____

Veins, arteries, and capillaries are the blood vessels that form the fantastic highway system in your body.

Write **vein, artery,** or **capillary** in front of the statement that best describes the type of blood vessel.

1. _____ carries blood away from the heart
2. _____ carries blood back to the heart
3. _____ is the tiniest blood vessel
4. _____ carries oxygen-rich blood
5. _____ connects the veins and arteries

Your blood is the vehicle that travels this highway. It transports oxygen, carbon dioxide, food, and waste. Your blood also fights infection and clots to prevent excessive blood loss.

To find out more about blood, do the crossword.

Across

2. Red blood cells are made in _____ marrow.
3. Blood plasma is clear liquid. It is 90 per cent _____.
4. Platelets prevent blood loss by forming a _____.
6. Hemoglobin carries _____ to the cells and takes carbon dioxide away from the cells.

Down

1. When you get a cut, white cells fight against _____.
4. Hemoglobin gives blood its red _____.
5. Hemoglobin is part of the _____ blood cells.

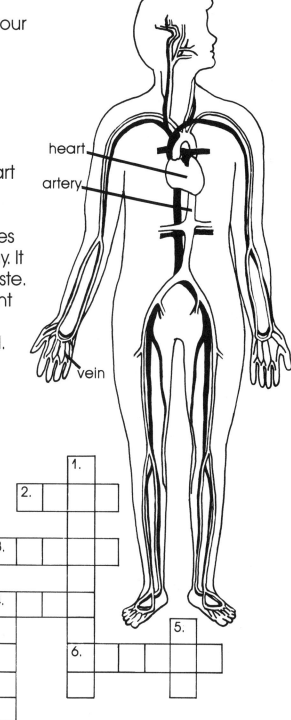

heart
artery
vein

Find Out

Thousands of people suffer from heart attacks each year. What causes heart attacks? What are some steps people can take to decrease the chance of heart attack?

Team Work

Name _____

Your heart is really two pumps that work together like a team. The right side of your heart takes dirty, carbon dioxide-filled blood in through the **right atrium** and **right ventricle.** It then pumps it through the **pulmonary artery** into your lungs. The blood is filled with oxygen in the lungs and passes through the **pulmonary vein** and into the **left atrium** and **left ventricle** on the left side of the heart. The left side of the heart then pumps this rich, oxygen-filled blood through the main artery of the body, called the **aorta**, to all the parts of your body.

Use arrows to trace the path of the blood.
Color the part of the heart filled with dirty, carbon dioxide-filled blood in blue.
Color the areas filled with oxygen-rich blood in red.

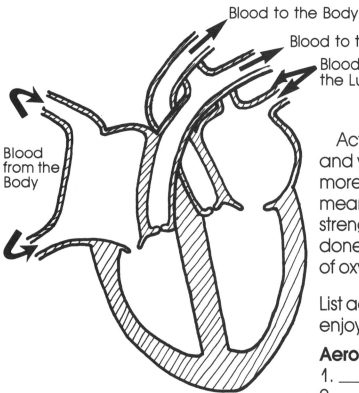

Blood to the Body

Blood to the Lungs

Blood from the Lungs

Blood from the Body

Activities that make you breathe deeper and your heart beat faster for 5 minutes or more are called **aerobic** activities. Aerobic means "using oxygen." These activities help strengthen your heart. Activities that are done quickly and don't require new supplies of oxygen are called **anaerobic** activities.

List aerobic and anaerobic activities that you enjoy.

Aerobic	**Anaerobic**
1. _____	1. _____
2. _____	2. _____
3. _____	3. _____
4. _____	4. _____
5. _____	5. _____

Find Out

For each kilogram of extra fat, your body is supplied with 580 km of blood vessels through which your heart must pump blood. If a person is 4 kg overweight, how much further would the heart have to pump blood? How could too much excess fat be harmful?

Pick Up the Beat

Name _____

Your pulse is caused by the stopping and starting of the blood as it rushes through your arteries. You can feel your pulse at any spot an artery is near the surface of the skin. These spots are called **pulse points.** One pulse point is located on the inside of your wrist.

Name some other pulse points.

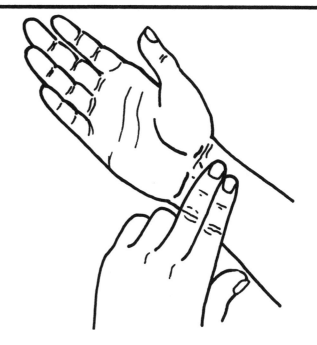

_____

_____

_____

Your pulse rate changes during different kinds of activity. Check your pulse rate after doing these activities.

Activity	Pulse rate for 15 seconds	Multiply by 4	Pulse rate for 1 minute
sitting			
hopping 25 times			
hopping 100 times			
lying down			

How does your pulse rate change during exercise?

_____

Why do you think your pulse rate changes during exercise?

_____

Find Out

How does body size affect pulse rate? Check the pulse rates for people of different sizes.

Respiratory System

Name _____

Your breathing, or respiratory, system is made of many parts. Solve the respiratory riddles using the word bank.

1. "I'm the windpipe that brings fresh air to your lungs." _____
2. "There are 600 million of us tiny air sacs in your lungs." _____
3. "Tra-la-la. I'm your voice box." _____
4. "We branch to the left and right from your windpipe." _____
5. "I enter your blood with each breath of fresh air." _____
6. "I help squeeze the air out of your lungs." _____

Label the diagram using the words from the word bank.

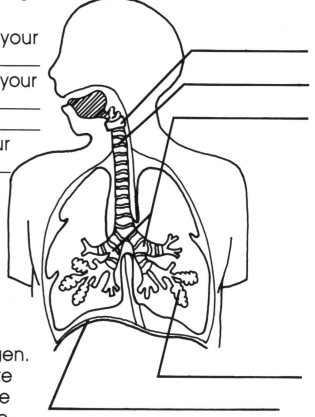

During exercise your body needs more oxygen. Your brain signals your lungs to breathe more quickly and take deeper breaths. Look at the results of the experiment below to answer the questions. Complete the chart.

Activity	Air in each breath (volume)	×	Number of breaths per minute	=	Air in lungs each minute
reading	.5 liters	×	16	=	
walking	1 liter	×	25	=	
playing basketball	2 liters	×	60	=	

Word Bank

alveoli
bronchial tubes
diaphragm
larynx
oxygen
trachea

Which activity makes you breathe fastest? _____
Which activity requires the most oxygen? _____
How much more air per minute does walking take than reading? _____

Digestive System

Use your science book or another source to help label the parts of the digestive system. Use words from the word bank.

This tastes food and moves it around in your mouth to be broken down by the teeth and saliva.

Food travels down this tube from the mouth to the stomach.

This organ produces the bile which helps break down fats.

Bile produced by the liver is stored here.

This is the first section of the small intestine. Food enters here after leaving the stomach. Digestion is still occurring.

This organ has no function in your body.

Saliva is produced here. Saliva starts changing starches into sugar while still in the mouth.

Food is stored here for 3-4 hours while digestion is occurring.

Produces digestive juices to help break down food in the small intestine.

Digestion is completed here. Nutrients are removed from food and enter the blood stream.

Solid material which is not used by the body is stored here for at least 24 hours. Water is removed during that time.

Waste (solid material which has not been digested) is stored here until ready to exit the body.

Waste exits the system through this body opening.

Word Bank

pancreas	large intestine	salivary glands
stomach	esophagus	gall bladder
liver	duodenum	rectum
appendix	small intestine	anus
tongue		

Keep It Covered

Name _____

Your skin does more than cover your body. Your skin does three important jobs. It helps keep your body cool and comfortable. It is a sensor that warns you of danger. And it provides protection from dirt and bacteria.

Label the parts of the cross-section of the skin using words from the word bank. Use your science book or another source to help.

Word Bank

pore
hair
nerve
oil gland
sweat gland
blood vessel
epidermis
dermis

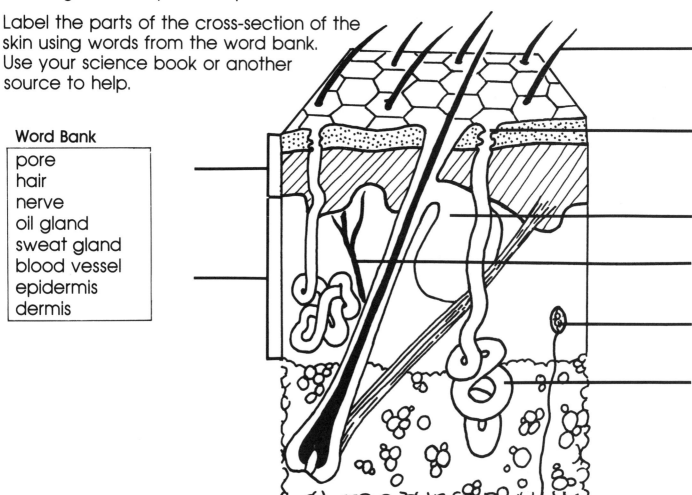

How does your skin help you in the following situations?

heat _____

dirt _____

pain _____

Fun Fact

Your skin is the thickest where the wear is the heaviest. The skin on the soles of your feet may be almost 5 mm thick and only .05 mm thick over the eye.

The Body's Camera

Name _____

Use your science book or another source to help.

Label the parts of the eye with terms from the word bank.

Word Bank

lens	pupil
cornea	retina
optic nerve	sclera
iris	vitreous humor

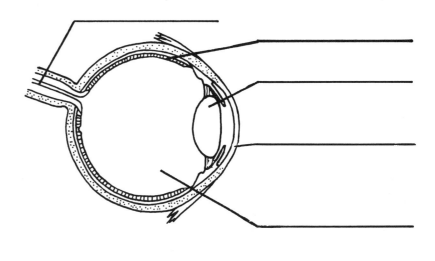

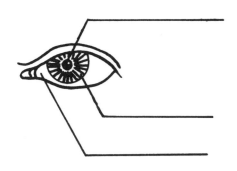

Complete the word puzzle using some of the words from the word bank.

Across
3. Dark area which changes size with the amount of light
5. Colored part of the eye
7. White covering of the eye
8. The clear jelly-like humor in the eye

Down
1. Transparent window of the eye
2. The nerve which sends light stimulus to the brain
4. Focuses light onto the retina
6. Sensitive area containing rods and cones

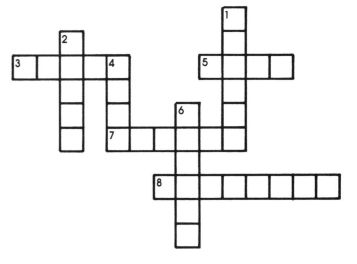

Something Special

Your retina is made up of light-sensitive cells that can be stimulated by pressure. Close your eyes and very gently press on them. The stars that you are seeing are called pressure flashes.

Catching Good Vibes

Name _____

Use your science book or another source to help.

Complete the following sentences using words from the word bank.

The car honks its horn. The sound waves are collected by your _____ and travel down the _____. The sound strikes the _____ causing the tight skin to vibrate. Three tiny bones called the _____, _____, and _____ magnify and send the sound to the inner ear. The sound travels to the _____, a coiled, snail-shaped passage filled with liquid and nerve hairs. The nerve hairs send signals through the _____ to the brain.

Label the parts of the ear using words from the word bank.

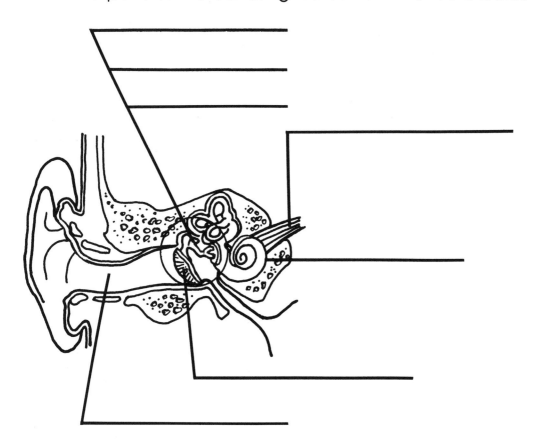

Word Bank

auricle
ear drum
auditory canal
auditory nerve
hammer
anvil
stirrup
cochlea

Something Special

Answer these riddles.
Which part of your ear has the most rhythm?
What pierces your ears without leaving holes?

Joe's Tooth: The Inside Story

Name _____

Use your science book or another source to help.

Word Bank

neck
root
crown
cementum
enamel
pulp
dentin

Label the inside parts of Joe's tooth using words from the word bank.

Label the outside parts of Joe's tooth using words from the word bank.

Complete the puzzle using words from the word bank.

Across

2. The outer covering of the tooth's roots
4. The hard, bone-like layer of the tooth
7. The part of the tooth located above the gum

Down

1. Soft tissues, blood vessels, and nerves that fill the inside space of the tooth
3. The tough, outer layer of the tooth
5. The part of the tooth between the crown and the root
6. The part of the tooth embedded in the jaw

Find Out

We all know that we should brush our teeth after every meal. But did you know that some foods can help keep your teeth clean? What are some of these "natural" toothbrushes?

Nibblers and Chompers

Name _____

Use your science book or another source to help.
Fill in the spaces with words from the word bank.

You have four kinds of _____ in your mouth, each with a special job. The large, front teeth are called _____. The incisors are the nippers that help you bite into an apple. The sharp pointy teeth are _____. Canines are used to tear food, like when you chew meat off a bone. The _____ are large teeth with two points. The _____ are the large, flat teeth in the back of your mouth. Both the bicuspids and molars are the "millstones" used for grinding food.

Label the teeth on the diagram by printing the following letters on the teeth:
I = Incisors   C = Canines   B = Bicuspids   M = Molars

Word Bank

canines
bicuspids
incisors
molars
teeth

Adult's Upper Teeth

Adult's Lower Teeth

You probably don't have as many teeth as shown in the diagram because you are still growing. As your jaw grows bigger, it makes room for new teeth.

Fill in the following chart.

Type of Teeth	Total Number of Teeth (upper and lower) Adult	You	Type of Chewing
Incisors			
Canines			
Bicuspids			
Molars			

Total Number of Adult Teeth = _____

Find Out

What are carnivores, herbivores, and omnivores? What kind of teeth do each of these have? Which one are you?

Cough! Cough!

Name _____

What makes your heart beat faster, replaces the oxygen in your blood with carbon monoxide, makes your blood pressure shoot up, and leaves deadly chemicals in your body–and all in just three seconds? If you answered, "cigarettes," then you are right.

When you inhale smoke, it travels down your windpipe and into your bronchial tubes. These tubes are covered with hair-like parts called **cilia.** The cilia move back and forth, trying to sweep the smoke dust back up the throat. Cough! Cough! The dust and dirt are out of your body. But cigarette smoke stops these hairs from doing their work. As a result, your lungs become lined with tar. This tar contains chemicals that are harmful to your body.

Cough! Cough! Is your body trying to tell you something?

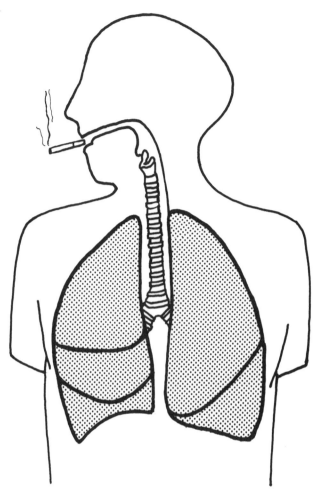

What are three excuses people use for smoking?
1. _____
2. _____
3. _____
What are three reasons why people should not smoke?
1. _____
2. _____
3. _____

✻ on the back

Something Special

Have you ever noticed ads for cigarettes in magazines and on billboards? What is the ad trying to tell you about smoking? Design an advertisement that discourages people from smoking.

49

Your Body and Medicine

Name _____

Drugs can be used as medicine to treat an illness or relieve pain. No one ever knows for sure how your body will respond to any drug. Drugs may cause harmful side effects. If you take an aspirin tablet for a headache, it may relieve your headache, but you might develop an upset stomach or become sleepy.

Drugs that can be bought in a drug store or supermarket are called "over-the-counter" drugs. These drugs may be bought without a doctor's permission. "Prescription" drugs are drugs that are controlled closely by the federal government and may be only bought with a doctor's permission. When using prescription and over-the-counter drugs, you should always read the label carefully.

Study the cough syrup label on this page and answer the questions.

1. Why would someone want to use this medicine? _____

2. How many teaspoons may a 10-year-old take? How often?

   _____

3. How many teaspoons may a 10-year-old take in 24 hours?

   _____

4. How many teaspoons should an adult take every 4 hours?

   _____

For Coughs Due to Cold and Flu
DIRECTIONS: ADULTS (12 years and over) 2 teaspoons every 4 hours, not to exceed 12 teaspoons in 24 hours. CHILDREN (6 to 11 years) 1 teaspoon every 4 hours, not to exceed 6 teaspoons in 24 hours.
WARNINGS AND CAUTIONS: KEEP OUT OF THE REACH OF CHILDREN
• Do not exceed recommended dosage because at higher doses, nervousness, dizziness, or sleeplessness may occur.
• Do not give this product to children under six years except with the advice and supervision of a physician.
• Consult a physician if symptoms persist for more than one week.
• Take only as your physician directs if you have a cough or high fever.

5. What should someone do if they still have a bad cough after 1 week?

   _____

6. What warning is given to people who have a high fever? _____

   _____

WARNING

Medicines can be helpful or harmful. They should never be taken without your parent's knowledge and supervision.

Puzzling Theory

Name _____

Many scientists accept the theory that the continents were at one time joined together as a single land mass called **Pangaea,** meaning "all the world."

Pangaea

- Cut out the shapes of the continents and their continental shelves. Place the west coast of Africa next to the east coast of South America. Try to fit the other continents next to Africa and South America. Glue all of them on a separate sheet of paper to form Pangaea.

1. Do all the continents fit together to form one land mass?_____
2. Which continents seem to fit together? _____
   _____
   _____

3. What do you think happened to the shape of the continents as they formed over a period of 200 million years? _____
   _____

Continents Today

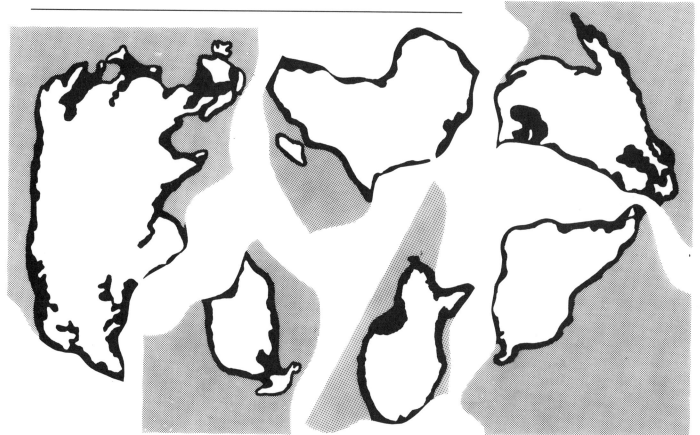

53   IF8759 Science Enrichment

Land Beneath the Ocean

Name _____

The land beneath the ocean has features that are very similar to those that you would see if you traveled across North America.

- Study the picture of the ocean floor. First label the picture and then the descriptions below, using the words from the word bank.

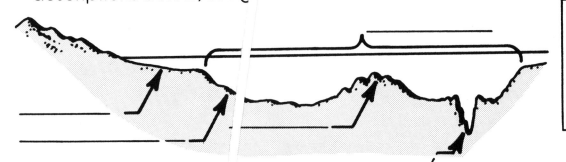

Word Bank
mid-ocean ridge
continental slope
continental shelf
ocean basin
trench

1. _____ A narrow, deep valley in the ocean basin.

2. _____ A steep incline at the edge of the continental shelf.

3. _____ A chain of mountains on the ocean floor.

4. _____ The part of the ocean floor nearest the continents.

5. _____ The deepest part of the ocean which contains valleys, plains, and mountains.

Many mountains on the mid-ocean ridges are almost 7,000 meters high, but still don't reach the surface of the ocean.

6. What is formed when an underwater mountain reaches the ocean's surface? _____

7. Give an example for number 6. _____

_____

8. Most commercial fishermen do not fish beyond the continental shelf. Why do you think this is so? _____

_____

Find Out

The Mariana Trench in the Pacific Ocean is nearly 11,000 meters deep. Mt. Everest is the highest mountain on earth, but is it higher than the Mariana Trench is deep? How does it compare in size?

"Ping-Ping"

Name _____

The depth of the ocean can be measured using a device called an echo sounder. A sound, "ping," is sent from a ship to the ocean floor. The length of time it takes for the "ping" to strike the ocean floor and bounce back to the ship is recorded. Sound travels in water at a speed of 1,500 meters per second. If a ping takes 6 seconds for a round trip, then a one way trip must take 3 seconds. The depth of the ocean at that point must be 4,500 m (3 sec. x 1,500 m/sec. = 4,500 m).

1. Find the various depths of the ocean using the "ping" soundings on this chart.

2. Using the depths you have listed on the chart, graph your results on the chart below. Connect the points to make a profile of the ocean floor.

3. Put a ✱ on the deep ocean trench.

4. Put an **X** on the continental slope.

5. Put an **M** on the undersea mountain.

Sounding	Time (sec.)		Speed (m/sec.)		Depth (m)
1	.4	X	1,500	=	600
2	.4	X	1,500	=	600
3	3	X	1,500	=	
4	2.6	X	1,500	=	3,900
5	3	X	1,500	=	
6	2	X	1,500	=	
7	1	X	1,500	=	
8	2	X	1,500	=	
9	3	X	1,500	=	
10	3.4	X	1,500	=	5,100
11	2	X	1,500	=	
12	7	X	1,500	=	
13	1	X	1,500	=	

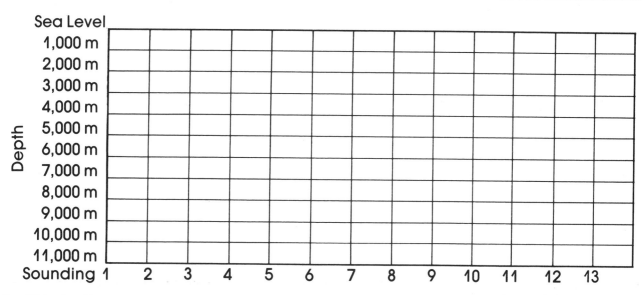

Fun Fact

Only 5% of the world's marine animals live below 1,000 m, in the sea's eternal darkness where sunlight cannot penetrate.

Fire Rocks

Name _____

Deep inside the earth the intense heat causes some rocks to melt. This molten rock, called **magma,** rises toward the surface of the earth because it is less dense than solid rock. Magma that flows onto the earth's surface is called **lava.** Some magma cools before it reaches the earth's surface, forming **igneous** rocks.

Many different types of igneous rocks can be formed, depending on how fast the magma or lava cools. When melted rock cools quickly, very small crystals are formed, causing the new rock to appear glassy. When molten rock cools slowly, large crystals are formed.

- Listed in the word bank are some common igneous rocks. Solve the puzzle, matching each rock with its description. Use what you have read above and information from other sources.

1. Melted rock that comes out of the earth.
2. Melted rock that cooled quickly, forming a black, glassy rock.
3. Greenish-black rock, formed from lava that flowed slowly over the surface.
4. Formed from lava that cooled with hot gases trapped inside, causing it to be filled with air holes.
5. Melted rock below the earth's surface.
6. Magma that cooled slowly, forming large crystals.
7. Lava that cooled slowly, forming large crystals.

Word Bank

pumice	gabbro
granite	magma
lava	obsidian
basalt	

1.__ __ __ __
2.__ __ __ __ __ __ __ __
3.__ __ __ __ __
4.__ __ __ __ __
5.__ __ __ __ __ __
6.__ __ __ __ __ __
7.__ __ __ __ __ __

- The hidden word: What do you call a mountain formed by cooled lava? _____

Something Special

It's fun to grow crystals. Rock candy is actually giant sugar crystals. Ask your librarian to help you find a recipe for growing your own super rock candy crystals.

 IF8759 Science Enrichment

Stones of Sand

Name _____

As rivers flow to the sea, they may carry mud, sand, pebbles, and boulders along the way. The river drops this material, called **sediment,** into the sea. As layers of sediment build up over a period of many years, the great pressure of all these layers changes the sediment into **sedimentary rock.**

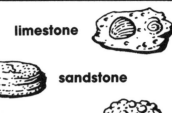

limestone

sandstone

conglomerate

Many different types of sedimentary rock can be formed, depending on the material that is found in the sediment. If the layer of sediment contains large amounts of sand, what kind of rock do you think will be formed? Of course, it will be sandstone.

- Use what you have read above and your science book to help you match the sedimentary rocks with their description.

____ 1. Layers and layers of sand are deposited on the sea bottom to form this rock.

____ 2. A mixture of sand and small pebbles is "cemented" together to form this rock.

____ 3. Living plants in a swamp are covered with sediment and pressed, eventually forming this valuable source of energy.

a. sandstone
b. shale
c. limestone
d. conglomerate
e. coal

____ 4. Small sea animals and shells are pressed into this kind of rock.

____ 5. Layers of mud form the most common type of sedimentary rock.

- Sediments settle at different rates of speed. Number these elements in the order that they would settle.

____ pebbles   ____ boulders   ____ sand

- What causes sediment to change into hard rock? _____
_____

- Where would you expect to find sedimentary rocks? _____
_____

Fun Fact

As the Mississippi River flows, it carries enough rock <u>each</u> <u>day</u> to fill 40,000 railroad cars.

Changing Rocks

Name _____

With enough pressure and heat, sedimentary and igneous rock can be changed into a new rock. This new kind of rock is called **metamorphic,** which means "changed in form."

There are a number of ways that metamorphic rock can be formed. One way is when rocks that are buried deep under the earth's surface are flattened by the great pressure from above them. An example of this is when granite is changed into gneiss. Look carefully at the pictures. How has the appearance of the granite changed?

granite

gneiss

Rock Cycle

sedimentary

igneous

metamorphic

magma

The changing of rocks is an ongoing cycle. Look closely at the rock cycle diagram. This cycle shows how rock material is mixed and re-used again and again.

Unscramble the terms to show examples of how igneous and sedimentary rocks can change into metamorphic rock.

1. _____ changes _____
   H E S A L   into   T A L E S

2. _____ changes _____
   T R I N E G A   into   S I N E G S

3. _____ changes _____
   M O E S T E L N I   into   B E L M A R

4. _____ changes _____
   T E N O S D A N S   into   Q U I T A Z E T R

- What three types of rock can an igneous rock change into? _____

- What must happen to an igneous rock before it changes into a sedimentary rock? _____

Find Out

Where is metamorphic rock used in your school? home? community?

Testing Minerals

Name _____

All minerals have certain characteristics, or properties, which distinguish them from other minerals. Minerals can be identified by the testing of these properties. A scratch test is used to determine the property of **hardness.** Minerals are rated on a scale of one to ten — one is the softest and ten the hardest.

Other properties are also tested. Some of the more common properties that we test are **color** and **luster.** Luster is the way a mineral reflects light.

It usually takes many more than the three properties mentioned to identify a mineral, but let's try our skill using only these three properties. (Caution: Some minerals can pass more than one test.)

Hardness Number	Test	Mineral
1	Fingernail scratches it easily	talc
2	Fingernail barely scratches it	gypsum/kaolinite
3	Copper penny scratches it	calcite/mica
4	Glass scratches it easily	fluorite
5	Steel knife will scratch it easily	apatite/hornblend
6	It will scratch glass	feldspar
7	It will scratch a steel knife	quartz
8	It will scratch a steel file	topaz
9	It will scratch topaz	corundum
10	It will scratch corundum	diamond

Color	
White:	quartz, feldspar, calcite, mica, gypsum, kaolinite, talc
Yellow:	quartz, kaolinite
Black:	hornblend, mica
Gray:	feldspar, gypsum, talc
Colorless:	quartz, calcite, gypsum

Luster	
Glassy:	quartz, feldspar, hornblend, gypsum
Pearly:	calcite, mica, gypsum, talc
Dull:	kaolinite

1.
Glassy
Colorless
It will scratch glass.
_____

2.
Pearly
Colorless
Copper penny scratches it.
_____

3.
Pearly
Black
Copper penny scratches it.
_____

4.
Dull
Yellow
Fingernail barely scratches it.
_____

5.
Glassy
Gray
It will scratch glass.
_____

6.
Glassy
Gray
Fingernail barely scratches it.
_____

7.
Glassy
Black
Steel knife will scratch it.
_____

8.
Pearly
White
Fingernail scratches it easily.
_____

It's California's Fault!

Name _____

There are many cracks in the earth's bedrock. These cracks are called **faults.** One kind of fault is called a **strike-slip fault.** The rock along one side of the fault moves horizontally in one direction, while the facing rock moves in the opposite direction. Other times, the bedrock on one side of the fault moves upward, while the other side moves down. This is called a **dip-slip fault.**

The San Andreas Fault is a large strike-slip fault that runs along the coast of California. This famous fault and other smaller faults that form the San Andreas Fault System have been the source of many earthquakes.

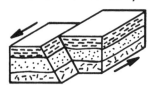
_____

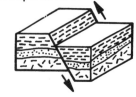
_____

1. Label the two types of faults using the words in bold above.

2. On which side of the San Andreas Fault is San Francisco? _____

3. On which side of the San Andreas Fault is Santa Cruz? _____

4. The San Andreas Fault's movement has been measured to be as much as 5 cm per year. What might happen to these two cities a million years from now? _____

_____

5. Many earthquakes occur along the San Andreas Fault. What are some things people can do to protect themselves from earthquakes? _____

_____

Fantastic Fact

During the 1906 San Francisco earthquake, roads, fences, and rows of trees that crossed the fault were shifted several meters. One road was shifted almost 7 meters!

Shake, Rattle, and Roll!

Name _____

An earthquake is a movement in the earth's crust. The large blocks of rock along a fault (a crack in the earth) slip past each other. As the blocks of rock slide, their sides may become locked. The strain builds and then becomes too great, causing the rocks to quickly slip past each other. The result is an earthquake. From the origin of the earthquake, called the **focus,** waves, or vibrations, move out in all directions.

Earthquakes are recorded on a sensitive instrument called a **seismograph.** The strength of the earthquake is measured on a scale of 1 to 10, with 10 being the strongest. This scale is called the **Richter Scale.**

| Mexico City — 2,600 km |
| Denver   — 1,400 km |
| Vancouver   — 1,600 km |

• Seismographs in three cities were able to record the same earthquake. The data showed that the focus of the earthquake was located at different distances from each of the cities. For each city, set your compass for the distance indicated. Draw a circle using the city as its center. Mark the focus by placing an **X** on the map where the three circles meet.

1. Where do earthquakes usually occur?_____
_____

2. Why might some earthquakes be stronger than others? _____
_____

3. Earthquakes can be felt for great distances, but where is the most damage usually done? _____
_____

Fantastic Fact

The Richter Scale measures the strength of an earthquake on a scale of 1 to 10. However, an earthquake with a reading of 2 is not twice as strong as a 1, but 32 times as strong. That means that the 1906 San Francisco earthquake, which measured 8.3, was 1 million times stronger than a weak earthquake that measures 4.2 on the Richter Scale.

 IF8759 Science Enrichment

Ring of Fire

Name _____

Deep inside the earth, melted rock called **magma** moves toward the earth's surface. When the magma reaches the surface, it is called **lava.**

In a volcano, the magma travels through a tube-like passageway called a **conduit,** until it reaches an opening in the earth's surface, called a **vent.** This vent may be in the top of the mountain or it could be a **side vent**. Sometimes the lava flows out gently, but other times it may explode violently.

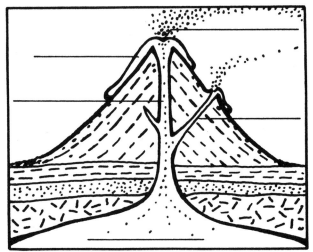

Volcanoes can occur wherever there is a deep crack in the earth's surface. Most volcanoes occur in a large belt that encircles the Pacific Ocean. This belt is called the **Ring of Fire.**

- Label the parts of the volcano using the words found in bold above.
- Many kinds of material may come out of a volcano. Complete the word puzzle using the clues and the words from the word bank.

1. Rocks with sharp corners that are blown out from the inside of a volcano.

2. Lava blown into the air, cools into small coarse pieces of rock which are puffed up by gas.

3. Magma that has reached the surface.

4. Lava that is blown apart by gases into light particles that can float in the air.

5. Ash mixed with rain, forming a cement-like rock.

6. Volcanic material that cools into a coarse rock containing many air bubbles, enabling the rock to float in water.

Word Bank

lava	pumice	blocks
gases	tuff	cinder
	ash	

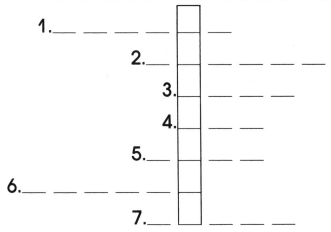

7. Carbon dioxide, sulfur dioxide, and steam are examples of these.

- Find the hidden name in the word puzzle of the famous active volcano that draws thousands of visitors to the island of Hawaii each year.

Mountain Building

Name _____

  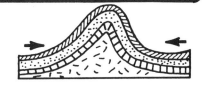

_____   _____   _____

Mammoth mountains can be found in many places throughout the world. How are these mountains formed?

Most mountains are formed when continental plates collide with each other. The force of the plates pushing against each other causes the crust to bulge up higher and higher, until "waves" of mountains are formed. The mountains that are formed this way are called **folded mountains.**

Other mountains are formed along faults. Along one side of the fault, the block of crust moves up. Along the other side of the fault, the block of crust moves down. The mountains that are formed from this are called **fault-block mountains.**

A third type of mountain, formed much in the same way folded mountains are, is a **dome mountain.** A bulge is formed. However, the bulge is caused by magma from the earth's mantle pushing against the crust.

1. Label the drawings of mountain types using the words in bold.

2. What is the main difference between a folded mountain and a fault-block mountain? _____

_____

3. What are two forces that form mountains? _____

_____

Mountain	Height	Location
McKinley	6,194 m	Alaska
Washington	1,916 m	New Hampshire
Shasta	4,316 m	California
Logan	6,050 m	Canada
Pike's Peak	4,300 m	Colorado

4. The two highest peaks in North America are listed on the chart. Name them and give their heights.

_____

_____

5. Make a bar graph using the information on the chart. Put the height in meters on the vertical axis, and the name of the mountain on the horizontal axis.

Fun Fact

The Himalaya Mountains of Tibet are the highest mountains on Earth. They were formed 40 million years ago when India drifted away from the east coast of Africa and crashed into Eurasia, piling up the Himalayas which are still growing today.

Natural Fountains

Name _____

Geysers, those spectacular natural fountains of spurting hot water, are actually a special kind of hot spring.

Water from rain and snow seeps thousands of meters underground. There the water is heated to 204° or higher, a temperature far above the boiling point of water. This superheated water expands and rises to the surface, where the steam bubbles escape. But from time to time, the bubbles become too abundant to pass up through the water. When this happens, so much steam builds up that the water actually explodes out of a vent in the ground, rising anywhere from 1 m to 60 m into the air.

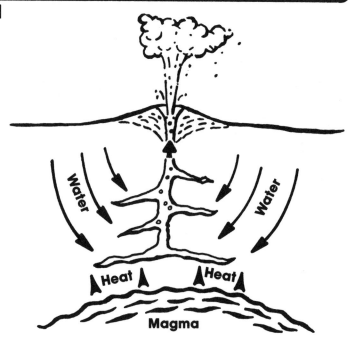

Yellowstone National Park is known for its geysers and hot springs. Listed below are a few of those geysers.

Geyser	Height	Duration	Interval
Artemisia	9 m	13-15 min.	24-30 hrs.
Beehive	45 m	5-8 min.	2-5 days
Great Fountain	60 m	35-60 min.	5-17 hrs.
Grotto	12 m	1-2 hrs.	1-12 hrs.
Lion	18 m	4 min.	1-2 hrs.
Old Faithful	56 m	2-5 min.	33-95 min.
Riverside	23 m	20 min.	6-9 hrs.
Steady	5 m	steady	steady

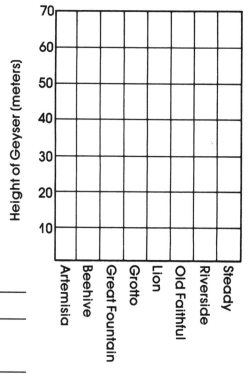

1. Graph the height of each geyser.

2. Which geyser erupts the most often? _____

3. Which geyser erupts the least often? _____

4. Which geyser could possibly have the shortest eruption? _____

5. Why do you think Old Faithful is the most popular geyser in the park? _____

Find Out

Some cities use these natural hot springs in many ways.
(1) How have the people of Reykjavik, Iceland used this geothermal energy?
(2) What are some other ways people can use this source of energy?

 IF8759 Science Enrichment

Rivers of Ice

Name _____

Ice —

Bedrock   Snow   Moraine

A large mass of snow and ice that lasts for years and years is called a **glacier.** Glaciers form over a period of years when more snow falls in the winter than melts in the summer. As the snow accumulates, the snow deep under the surface snow compresses into thick, dense ice. This ice, called **firn,** can be from 30 to 50 meters thick.

In mountainous regions, the downward pull of gravity on the ice causes the flow down the mountainside. As the solid glacier flows, it picks up rocks and stones. When the glacier melts, the rocks and stones are deposited in small mounds called **moraines.**

- The force of a glacier has left these glacial terms in a bit of a mess. Unscramble them. You may consult your science book or another resource book.

Glacier formed long smooth hills.

_ _ _ _ _ _ _ _
D M L R U N I S

Refrozen snowmelt in a glacier.

_ _ _ _
F N I R

Large crack in a glacier.

_ _ _ _ _ _ _ _
S R A C E S E V

Melted glacial ice.

_ _ _ _ _ _
M T W T
E A L E R

Small mound formed by the deposit of rocks from a melting glacier.

_ _ _ _ _ _ _
R O M I N A E

Winding ridge left by melting glacier.

_ _ _ _ _
K E R S E

Hollows in the land left by melting chunks of ice.

_ _ _ _ _ _ _
L E K E T T S

1. What are two reasons snow would stay on the ground year-round? _____

_____

2. What happens to snow packed down by a great force? _____

_____

3. Is there any evidence that glaciers once existed in your area? _____

Fun Fact
About three-fourths of all fresh water in the world—the equivalent of 60 years of precipitation over the entire globe—is stored in glacial ice.

       IF8759 Science Enrichment

3-D Geologic Map

Name _____

Create your own three-dimensional geologic map.

   (1) Make your own key using colors and symbols.
   (2) Color each rock formation according to your key.
   (3) Cut out the map.
   (4) Fold the map to form a box.
   (5) Glue the flaps on the inside of the box.

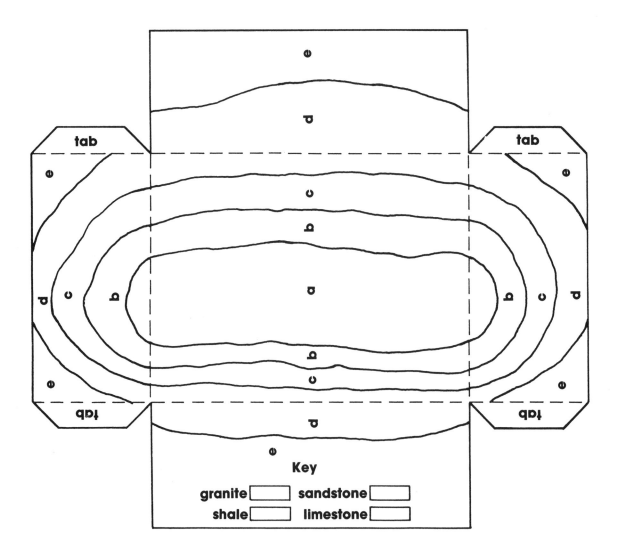

Key

granite [   ]   sandstone [   ]
shale [   ]   limestone [   ]

• Have you made an incline or a syncline? _____

Challenge

Make your own map of an incline. Maybe you could include a dike. You might want to make your map out of a sturdy material, such as tagboard.

Just Plain Dirt

Name _____

Soil is made of pieces of rocks and minerals that have been broken down by nature over a period of thousands of years.

Soil is found in three layers. The top layer, where plants usually grow, is called **topsoil.** The second layer, which contains pebbles, sand, and clay, is called **subsoil.** The bottom layer contains large rocks and is called **bedrock.**

• How is soil formed? _____

_____

• The foundation of a very large building often goes all the way down to the bedrock. Why? _____

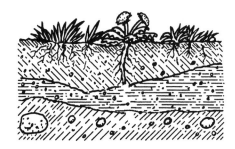

Soil	Structure	Properties
Sand	Small pieces of quartz	Does not hold water
Clay	Very small pieces of mineral other than quartz	Holds water very well
Loam	Sand, clay, and humus (decayed plants and animals)	Holds water yet drains

Tell what type of soil you would choose in each situation below. The chart will help you.

1. Garden _____ Why? _____

_____

2. Bottom of a man-made pond _____ Why? _____

_____

3. Bottom layer of soil in a landfill _____ Why? _____

_____

4. Soil under swings and slide on a playground _____ Why? _____

_____

5. Soil under the sod of a ball field _____ Why? _____

_____

Find Out

Investigate samples of soil found near your home and school. How fast do equal amounts of water percolate (drain) into the soil? Try some other tests of your own.

Earth Shattering Review

Name _____

Solve this puzzle using the word bank below.

Down

1. Small mound formed by a deposit of rocks from a glacier.
3. Movement in the earth's crust caused by the slipping of large blocks of rock along a fault.
6. Rocks formed by layers of sediment under great pressure.
8. Single land mass in the theory of continental drift.
9. Remains or imprints of organisms left in sedimentary rock.
10. A narrow, deep valley in the ocean basin.

Across

2. Rocks that are changed in form.
4. The thin outer layer of the earth.
5. Rocks formed by the cooling of magma.
7. The innermost layer of the earth.
9. A crack in the earth's bedrock.
11. Molten rock beneath the surface of the earth.
12. Layer of rock between the earth's core and crust.

Word Bank

magma	mantle	sedimentary	igneous
lava	crust	fossils	coal
moraine	earthquake	fault	trench
Pangaea	focus	metamorphic	core

IF8759 Science Enrichment

How Does the Earth Move?

Name _____

Hold on tight to your desk. You can't feel it, but you are traveling at a speed of 30 km per hour! The earth is actually traveling at this speed in a circular path around the sun. This path is called its **orbit.** Each complete orbit, or **revolution** around the sun, takes 365¼ days.

The earth has a second type of motion. It spins, or rotates, like a top about an imaginary line that runs from the North Pole to the South Pole. This imaginary line is called the earth's **axis.** Each complete **rotation** of the earth takes 24 hours. This motion gives us night and day.

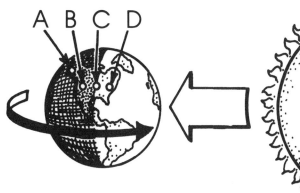

In the picture, City C is experiencing sunrise. Which city has had sunlight for about one hour?_____

Which cities are still dark?_____

Which city will be the next to experience sunrise? _____

1. Which movement of the earth gives us our 24-hour day?_____

2. Which movement of the earth gives us our 365¼ day year? _____

3. How many complete rotations has the earth made this month?_____

4. How many complete revolutions has the earth made since you were born?_____

Something Special

All of the planets in the Solar System revolve around the sun. Their orbits are not perfect circles. They revolve in an **ellipse.**

You can draw an ellipse. Place two straight pins about 8 cm apart in a piece of cardboard. Tie the ends of a 25 cm piece of string to the pins. Place your pencil inside the string. Keeping the string tight, draw an ellipse.

Make four different ellipses by changing the length of the string and the distance between the pins. How do the ellipses change?

IF8759 Science Enrichment

Reasons for the Seasons

Name _____

Do you know why it is hot in the summer and cold in the winter? Because the earth is tilted! The tilt of the earth causes different parts of the earth to get varying amounts of sunlight as it orbits the sun.

Let's take a quick look at the seasons for people living in the Northern Hemisphere. During the summer months, the North Pole is tilted toward the sun. The Northern Hemisphere receives more of the sun's direct rays causing the days to become warmer and the number of daylight hours to increase. Six months later the North Pole is tilted away from the sun. Then the days become colder and the number of daylight hours decreases.

Label the four seasons for the Northern Hemisphere on the diagram below.

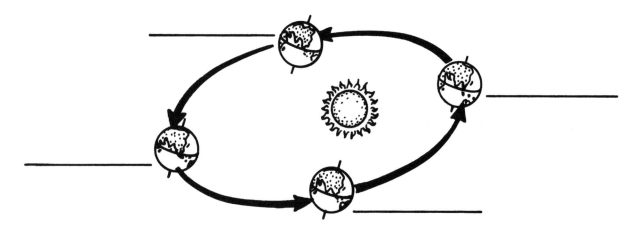

Many things are affected by the changing of the seasons. Complete the chart below using information for your region.

	Outdoor Clothing	Outdoor Activities	Average Daytime Temperature	Time It Gets Dark
Summer				
Fall				
Winter				
Spring				

Fun Fact

The sun is not exactly at the center of the earth's orbit. During the northern winter, the earth is more than four million kilometers closer to the sun than in the summer. This makes the northern winters warmer than the southern winters.

Our Moon

Name _____

On July 20, 1969, Neil Armstrong and Edwin Aldrin left the first footprints on the moon. The astronauts found our moon to be without air, water, plants, or any living things.

The moon is covered with billions of bowl-shaped holes called **craters.** Some are as small as soup bowls, and others are many kilometers in diameter. Scientists believe the craters were formed when objects traveling in space hit and dented the moon's surface.

When you look at the moon with a telescope, you will see large, flat, smoother areas. Early astronomers believed that these areas were oceans. They called the areas **maria,** which means "seas" in Latin. Actually, there is no water on the moon. Maria are dry lava beds that were formed by volcanic action on the moon about 3½ million years ago.

Pretend you are an astronaut preparing for a visit to the moon. Decide which items from the list below would be needed or not needed for your visit. Give your reasons.

Item	Needed	Not Needed	Reason
firewood			
signal whistle			
matches			
water			
raincoat			
lightweight equipment			
oxygen			
food			

Fun Fact

The moon's gravity is 1/6 of the earth's. A person weighing 54 kilograms on earth would weigh only 9 kilograms on the moon. Find your moon weight by dividing your earth weight by 6.

Earth weight _____ Moon weight _____

Changing Faces

Name _____

Everyone has heard about the man in the moon. You have probably even seen pictures of the moon's "face." Have you ever noticed that the moon's face appears to have different shapes at different times of the month? These changes in shape are called the moon's **phases.** Of course, the moon does not actually change shape, nor does it produce its own light. Do you know what accounts for the moon's shape and light?

As the moon revolves around the earth, we can see different amounts of the moon's lighted part. Study the drawing of the moon's different phases carefully.

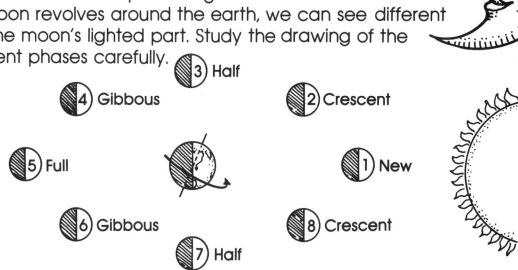

Draw each of the moon's phases as it will be seen from earth. Label each phase.

1	2	3	4
5	6	7	8

Waxing or Waning

As the moon "grows" from the new moon to the full moon, we say the moon is **waxing.** As it "shrinks" from full moon to new moon, we say it is **waning.** Label three of your drawings as waning and three as waxing.

Fun Fact

The moon's gravitational pull causes the continent of North America to rise as much as 15 cm when the moon passes over.

Space Shadows

Name _____

Crack! It's a high flyball. The sun is shining in the ballplayer's eyes. With one hand raised, the player blocks out the sun, and a shadow appears across his eyes. He can easily see the ball and make the catch.

Just like the ballplayer's outstretched hand, objects in space often cast shadows. Sometimes the moon passes between the earth and the sun. The moon slowly blocks out the sun's light, casting a shadow on the earth. The sky gets dark, the air cools, and for several minutes you can see the stars. This is a **solar eclipse.**

As the moon travels around the earth, sometimes the earth will cast a shadow on the moon. The full moon darkens as it moves into the earth's shadow. This eclipse, which will last for over an hour, is called a **lunar eclipse.**

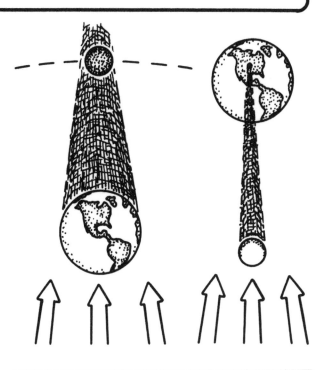

Draw the position of the moon and the shadows for both the solar and lunar eclipses. Label each picture.

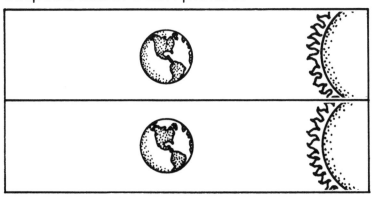

Complete the following chart by checking the correct box for each statement.	Lunar Eclipse	Solar Eclipse
earth casts a shadow		
moon casts a shadow		
takes place at night		
takes place during the day		
moon is blocked out		
sun is blocked out		
causes the sky to get dark		
causes the air to cool		

Something Special

Tribes in the South Pacific had an interesting way of explaining eclipses. They thought that angry gods would swallow the sun or moon and then almost immediately vomit their meal. The sun and moon would continue to shine.

Make up your own legend to explain why eclipses take place.

Exploring Our Solar System

Name _____

You can learn much about the planets in our Solar System by studying the table on this page. Use the information from the table to answer the questions.

Planet	Diameter	Distance from the Sun	Revolution	Rotation
Mercury	4,880 km	57,900,000 km	88 days	59 days
Venus	12,100 km	108,200,000 km	225 days	243 days
Earth	12,756 km	149,600,000 km	365 days	24 hours
Mars	6,794 km	228,000,000 km	687 days	24.5 hours
Jupiter	143,200 km	778,400,000 km	11.9 years	10 hours
Saturn	120,000 km	1,425,600,000 km	29.5 years	11 hours
Uranus	51,800 km	2,867,000,000 km	84 years	16 hours
Neptune	49,500 km	4,486,000,000 km	164 years	18.5 hours
Pluto	2,600 km	5,890,000,000 km	247 years	6.5 days

1. Which planet is closest to the sun?_____

2. Which planet is farthest from the sun? _____

3. Which planets are located between Earth and the sun?_____

_____

4. Which is the largest planet?_____

5. Which is the smallest planet? _____

6. What is the diameter of Earth? _____

7. How long does it take for Pluto to revolve around the sun? _____

8. Which planet takes the least time to revolve around the sun? _____

9. Which planet revolves around the sun in 365 days? _____

10. Which planet takes the longest to rotate? _____

11. Which planet is almost the same size as Earth? _____

12. Which planet is larger, Pluto or Mars? By how much?_____

Something Special

Here is an easy way to remember the names of the planets in the order of their distance from the sun. The first letter in each of the words represents one of the planets.

My Very Educated Mother Just Served Us Nine Pizzas

Earth's Nearest Neighbors

Name _____

With a roar of the giant rocket engines, we are pressed tightly to our seats. We are on our way to visit Earth's closest planet neighbors. Our journey takes us first to a planet that looks much like our moon with its craters. It is **Mercury**, the smallest of our neighboring planets. It is only one-half of Earth's size. There is no air on Mercury to block out the sun's extreme heat. This causes the surface temperature on Mercury to reach 400ºC.

As our spacecraft continues, we sight a planet that is almost the size of Earth. This is **Venus**, covered with a mist of swirling, yellow clouds. These clouds are made up of droplets of sulfuric acid. We cannot land here because the air is mostly carbon dioxide and the temperature is 470ºC.

Our spacecraft speeds past Earth, quickly approaching a red-colored planet about half the size of Earth. Its surface is dry and desert-like and covered with craters. This is **Mars**, with its violent dust storms. Be sure to keep an eye out for Martians! The temperature on the surface is 26ºC. But we won't see any life here because the air is 100 times thinner than Earth's and is 95 per cent carbon dioxide.

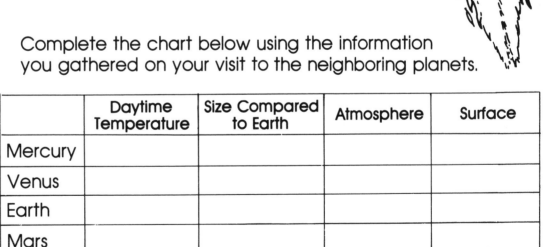

Complete the chart below using the information you gathered on your visit to the neighboring planets.

	Daytime Temperature	Size Compared to Earth	Atmosphere	Surface
Mercury				
Venus				
Earth				
Mars				

Fun Fact

Because Venus travels in an orbit inside the earth's orbit, it appears to us in phases. Its night side faces Earth every 584 days.

The Outer Planets

Name _____

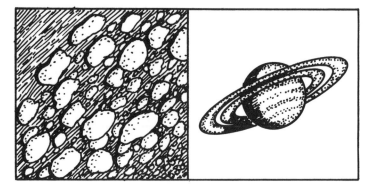

Our spacecraft pushes on to explore the two largest planets in our Solar System.

We are approaching the largest planet, **Jupiter.** It is eleven times wider than Earth. If it were hollow, it could hold 1,300 Earths inside! We can see Jupiter's rapidly changing bands of clouds and brilliant flashes of lightning. It is extremely warm; Jupiter gives off twice as much heat as it receives from the sun. The Great Red Spot on the surface is a tremendous storm, 14,000 km wide and 40,000 km long. It travels completely around the planet every six days. Beneath the thick clouds, Jupiter is a great, spinning ball of liquid ammonia and methane gases.

We are now approaching one of the most fantastic sights of our journey–the giant rings of **Saturn.** The rings sparkle in the sunlight as they circle the glowing, yellow planet. As we get closer to the rings, we notice that they are actually particles of ice and ice-covered rock orbiting the planet. The rings are over 65,000 km wide but only a few kilometers thick. Like Jupiter, Saturn seems to be covered with a thick covering of clouds. High winds are blowing, and the temperature in the clouds is -190°C.

1. Which is the largest planet in the Solar System?_____

2. Which is the second largest?_____

3. What are Saturn's great rings?_____

4. What is Jupiter's "Great Red Spot"?_____

5. How are Saturn and Jupiter alike?_____

   _____

6. Could you live on Jupiter? Why or why not? _____

   _____

Fun Fact

Even though Saturn is the second largest planet, it has the lowest density of all the planets. If you could put Saturn in a giant tub of water, it would float!

The Edge of the Solar System

Name _____

Three distant planets remain for us to visit before we head back to Earth. Very little is known about these planets because of their distance from the sun.

Our spaceship is approaching the greenish-blue planet of **Uranus.** It appears to be about four times the diameter of Earth. It has nine rings, much like Saturn's. The planet is covered with clouds that are made up of hydrogen, helium, and methane gas. As we leave Uranus, we can count five moons orbiting the planet.

We are now 4.5 billion kilometers from Earth and are approaching the eighth planet, **Neptune.** Neptune is similar in size to Uranus. It is also covered with a thick, cloud atmosphere of hydrogen and methane gas.

As we get nearer to **Pluto,** we are now at the edge of the Solar System. If we look back, our sun appears like a bright star in the sky. Pluto is so far away from the sun that the temperature is almost absolute zero, the point at which there is no heat at all!

Use the clues to fill in the puzzle and find the secret word.

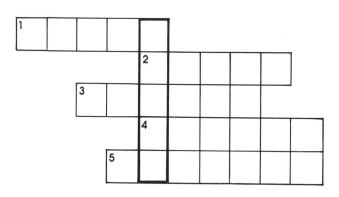

1. Uranus has five _____.
2. Planet farthest from the sun
3. Planet with nine rings
4. Neptune is covered with _____.
5. Eighth planet from the sun

The secret word is _____!

Find Out

Uranus lies on its side as it revolves around the sun once every 84 years. For 42 years, one pole is in the sunlight, and the other is in darkness. During the next 42 years, the conditions reverse. Where do the longest nights and days occur on Earth? When does it happen? Why does it happen?

 IF8759 Science Enrichment

Comets, Asteroids, and Meteors

Name _____

There are other objects in our Solar System besides planets, moons, and the sun. You might have seen some of them streaking by if you have ever stared at the evening sky.

Comets are like "dirty snowballs." A comet is made up of frozen gas (the snow) and dust particles (the dirt). It shines by reflecting the sun's light as it travels in a stretched-out orbit around the sun. As a comet gets closer to the sun, it melts and forms a "tail."

Between the orbits of Jupiter and Mars are thousands of rocky objects, called **asteroids,** orbiting the sun. Asteroids, some as large as 1,000 km long, are believed to be pieces of a planet that broke apart.

Meteors are streaks of light made by chunks of stone or metal traveling through Earth's atmosphere and burning up. If a meteor strikes the earth, it is called a meteorite. Some people call meteors "shooting stars."

Label the different parts of the Solar System: the sun, the planets, the comet, and the asteroids.

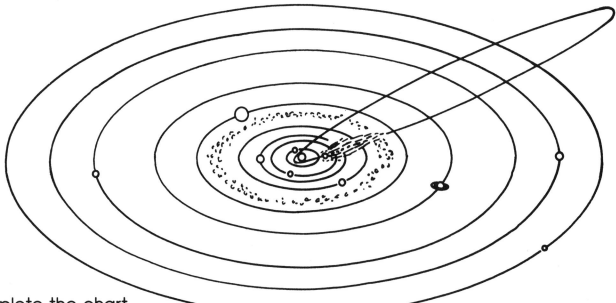

Complete the chart
by placing a (✓) in the appropriate box.

	Meteor	Asteroid	Comet
frozen ball of dust			
orbits the sun			
shooting star			
burns up in Earth's atmosphere			
orbits between Mars and Jupiter			
appears as a streak in the sky			
is visible in our sky			

Magnitude

Name _____

The stars that you see on a clear night seem to be closer than they really are. Light from the sun, the closest star to Earth, takes 8.3 minutes to reach us. Light from the next closest star, Proxima Centauri, takes 4.3 years to reach us. Proxima Centauri is not even visible without the aid of a telescope.

All of the stars in the sky do not look alike. The most visible difference is in the brightness of the stars. The measure of brightness is called **magnitude.** The magnitude of a star is determined by its size, distance from Earth, and its temperature.

Stars are balls of hot gases. The color of a star helps us determine its temperature. Red stars are the coldest stars, with a surface temperature of 3,000°C. The hottest stars that can be seen are blue stars. Their temperature is over 20,000°C. White stars are over 10,000°C. Our sun is a yellow star with a surface temperature of 5,500°C.

Use what you have learned about temperature and star color to color the stars.

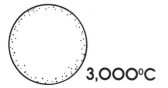 3,000°C   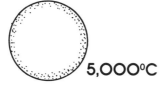 5,000°C    10,000°C   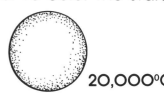 20,000°C

What three factors determine a star's magnitude?

_____   _____   _____

Two stars are the same color and distance from Earth, but their size is different. Which star will have the greater magnitude?_____

Use the information from the chart to make a graph showing the temperature of the four stars.

Star	Color	Temperature
Rigel	Blue-white	12,000°C
Sun	Yellow	5,500°C
Betelgeuse	Red	3,000°C
Sirius	White	10,500°C

13,000°C
11,000°C
9,000°C
7,000°C
5,000°C
3,000°C
1,000°C
0°C

Rigel   Sun   Betelgeuse   Sirius

A Star is Born

Name _____

Nobody has ever lived long enough to see a star being "born" and then "die." The changes in a star's life take place over billions of years. Let's look at the stages of a typical star.

A star is formed from a swirling **nebula,** or cloud of dust and gas, in space. The forces of gravity press the matter in the nebula together. When the matter is pressed tightly enough, it gets hotter and hotter, until a new star is born. This new star is large and cool–although cool is 3,000°C. The new star has a red glow.

If the star continues to compress, the matter may become one of several different colors. It may become blue, white, yellow, or red. In terms of star heat, this is hot, warm, lukewarm, or cool. Our sun is a yellow star. It is hotter than a red star, but cooler than a white star.

1. How long is the life span of a star?_____

2. What is a nebula?_____

3. What color is the sun?_____

4. Which color stars are hotter than our sun? Cooler than our sun?_____

_____

Number the stages of the birth of a star in the correct order.

_____ The matter in the young star continues to compress and get hotter.

_____ The nebula is a swirling mass of dust and gas.

_____ The newly born star is a cool 3,000°C.

_____ Gravity forces dust and gases of the nebula to press together.

_____ The star becomes a new color as it gets hotter.

Find Out

Our sun is a five billion year-old star that has been using up 4½ billion tons of hydrogen every second. How much hydrogen does the sun use in one day?

Star Death

Name _____

As stars get older, they go through changes. A star begins "old age" when its central core of hydrogen has become all helium. Its energy source is gone. Gravity squeezes the center core tight, while the outer layers begin to expand and cool to a dull red. The star becomes a **red giant.**

The outer layer forms a ring nebula that disappears into space leaving behind a super-collapsed core, about the size of a planet. The core becomes hotter as it collapses and forms a small, white star called a **white dwarf.** The white dwarf is so dense that a teaspoon of material would weigh almost one ton.

Because the white dwarf has no energy left, it grows dimmer and dimmer until it is a cold, black sphere called a **black dwarf.**

As you grow older, you can see changes over periods of months and years. You can't see the changes in stars. Stars change over periods of millions, and sometimes billions, of years.

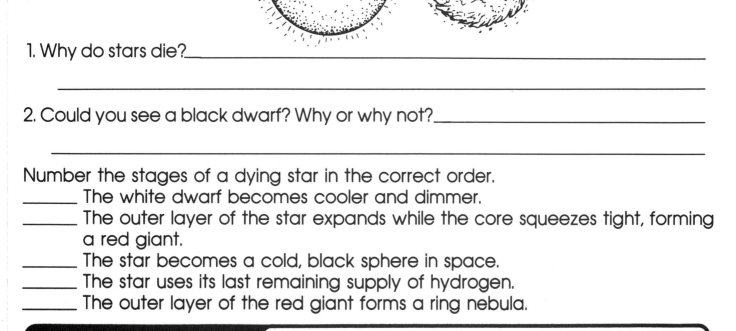

1. Why do stars die?_____

_____

2. Could you see a black dwarf? Why or why not?_____

_____

Number the stages of a dying star in the correct order.
_____ The white dwarf becomes cooler and dimmer.
_____ The outer layer of the star expands while the core squeezes tight, forming a red giant.
_____ The star becomes a cold, black sphere in space.
_____ The star uses its last remaining supply of hydrogen.
_____ The outer layer of the red giant forms a ring nebula.

Fun Fact

Sometimes massive stars explode leaving behind a super-dense core called a neutron star. The gravity is so strong on a neutron star, that the average person would weigh about 13½ billion tons if standing on the neutron star's surface!

Black Holes

Imagine a star with gravity so strong that nothing can escape from it, not even light. These stars are called **black holes.**

When a massive star begins to burn out, it collapses. A star ten times the size of our sun will shrink to a sphere about 60 km in diameter. It becomes so dense and the gravitational pull so strong, that the star disappears! Anything that passes close to it in space will be sucked in and never get out!

How do astronomers look for black holes if they can't be seen? They look indirectly. A black hole pulls in matter from nearby stars. As the matter disappears, it sends out strong bursts of x-rays. Astronomers look for these x-ray signals. The most promising candidate for a black hole is the x-ray source known as Cygnus X-1.

Secret Message

The black hole below has swallowed some of the planets of the Solar System. Shade in the names of the planets. The letters that are not shaded will help you solve the secret message.

S	A	T	U	R	N	I	J
F	B	L	A	C	K	H	U
P	O	M	A	R	S	L	P
L	V	E	N	U	S	E	I
U	S	R	E	X	A	I	T
T	S	C	T	N	T	O	E
O	B	U	O	D	U	Y	R
C	A	R	E	A	R	T	H
N	S	Y	E	E	N	T	H
E	U	R	A	N	U	S	M

— — ———— ——

— — — — —

— — — — — ,

— — — — — — —

— — — — — —

— — — — .

Something Special

Black holes seem almost like science fiction. Write a science fiction newspaper article using this headline.

STAR TIMES

Explorer XII Last Seen Near Cygnus X-1

IF8759 Science Enrichment

Pictures in the Stars

Name _____

Have you ever made pictures by drawing dot-to-dot? On a clear night, lie on your back and gaze up at the hundreds of twinkling stars. Try to imagine different pictures by drawing lines from star to star. Hundreds of years ago, people drew pictures with the stars in this same way. These pictures are called **constellations.**

Many of the constellations get their names from Greek mythology. One well-known constellation of the winter skies is Orion, the mighty hunter of Greek mythology.

We can use constellations to help locate special stars. The Big Dipper is a constellation that can help you locate Polaris, the North Star. With your eye, make an imaginary line from the two stars on the end of the Dipper's cup. This line will point to Polaris.

Big Dipper

Polaris

1. What is a constellation? _____

2. How can a constellation be helpful to the stargazer? _____

_____

Many constellations are hard to picture. Below are the four star patterns that are also shown above. Identify the constellations by their common name. Then connect the stars to form a new constellation of your own. Give this new constellation a name.

Common name_____
New name _____

Common name_____
New name _____

Common name_____
New name _____

Common name_____
New name _____

     IF8759 Science Enrichment

The Zodiac

Name _____

Ancient astronomers noticed that certain constellations always came up in the east just before sunrise. This was because they were found in the same path that was traced by the sun across the sky. The path made by these constellations actually formed a belt that circled around the heavens. This belt was divided into twelve equal parts, each containing one major constellation.

Most of the constellations that appeared in this belt were named after animals. The early Greeks called this belt **Zodiakos Kyklos,** or "circle of animals." We call it the **Zodiac** for short.

The Zodiac was eventually used by fortune-tellers, known as astrologers, to tell the fortune of a person born under a particular Zodiac sign. (Each Zodiac sign is associated with a specific time period in the year.) The reading by an astrologer is called a **horoscope.**

Circle the Latin names of the twelve constellations of the Zodiac in the wordsearch.

Word Bank

Aquarius	Libra
Aries	Pisces
Cancer	Sagittarius
Capricorn	Scorpio
Gemini	Taurus
Leo	Virgo

```
D C E C A N C E R F U
S A G I T T A R I U S
B Q S C O R P I O G G
A U Q U H P R T V A E
R A I V R I I A Z R M
U R S I P S C U T I I
L I B R A C O R O E N
J U K G L E R U W S I
O S N O M S N S L E O
```

Match each Latin name with its English translation.

_____	The Ram	_____	The Scales
_____	The Bull	_____	The Scorpion
_____	The Twins	_____	The Archer
_____	The Crab	_____	The Goat
_____	The Lion	_____	The Water Carrier
_____	The Virgin	_____	The Fish

Find Out

Astrology is a "pseudo-science." What is a pseudo-science? Can you name other pseudo-sciences?

Space Puzzle

Name _____

Use the clues and words from the word blank to complete the puzzle. Use the numbered letters to solve the riddle at the bottom of the page.

Word Bank

astronomer	fall	Mercury	Pluto	sun
axis	fusion	meteorite	red	
Centauri	hydrogen	moon	rotation	
Earth	maria	orbit	shuttle	

1. A star's energy comes from nuclear __ __ __ __ __ __ .
       ₁

2. The only planet with life is __ __ __ __ __ .
              ₂

3. The path of a planet around the sun is its __ __ __ __ __ .
                  ₃

4. Earth's largest satellite is the __ __ __ __ .
           ₄

5. The autumnal equinox is the first day of __ __ __ __ .
              ₅

6. The planet farthest away from the sun is __ __ __ __ __ .
                 ₆

7. The closest planet to the sun is __ __ __ __ __ __ __ .
               ₇

8. A meteor that lands on the earth is a __ __ __ __ __ __ __ __ __ .
                   ₈

9. A scientist who studies the Universe is an __ __ __ __ __ __ __ __ __ __ .
                 ₉

10. A star's fuel is __ __ __ __ __ __ __ __ .
          ₁₀

11. The star closest to the earth is the __ __ __ .
           ₁₁

12. Oceans on the moon are called __ __ __ __ __ .
               ₁₂

13. A space __ __ __ __ __ __ __ is a reusable space craft.
        ₁₃

14. The closest star to our solar system is Proxima __ __ __ __ __ __ __ __ .
                 ₁₄

15. The color of a dying star is __ __ __ .
            ₁₅

16. The spinning movement of a planet is its __ __ __ __ __ __ __ __ .
                ₁₆

17. The imaginary line from the North Pole to the South Pole is the Earth's

__ __ __ __ .
 ₁₇

Something Special

How do creatures from outer space drink their tea?

__ __ __ __   __ __ __ __ __   __ __ __ __ __ __ __ !!
1 2 3 4   5 6 7 8 9 10   11 12 13 14 15 16 17

What Is Weather?

Name _____

"Today it will be sunny and warm with increasing cloudiness in the late afternoon." The changing condition in the atmosphere (the layer of air that surrounds the earth) is called **weather.**

Weather is caused by the uneven heating of the atmosphere. For example, where the sun's rays strike the earth at a slant, the earth is heated less than where the sun's rays strike directly. Also, water and land absorb heat and cool off at different rates.

Energy from the sun, called **solar energy,** causes weather. Look at the picture. What happens to the sun's energy?

30% reflected by clouds and dust

10% reflected by the earth

20% absorbed by atmosphere

40% absorbed by the earth

1. Using the information from the picture, complete the circle graph to indicate what happens to the sun's energy.

   ▤ absorbed by the atmosphere

   ▨ _____

   ▦ _____

   ⊠ _____

Sun's Energy

North Pole

2. Look at the picture. At which point is the earth's surface heated more? Why?

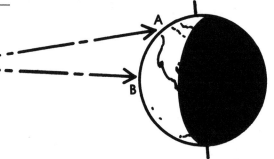

Sun

A

B

South Pole

_____

_____

_____

Something Special

Water and land (soil) absorb the sun's energy at different rates. Explain how you could prove this with a simple experiment.

Pop!

Have you ever felt your ears "pop" while riding down a large hill in a car? Your ears have sensed a change in **air pressure.**

Air pressure is the force of all the air in the atmosphere pushing down on the surface of the earth. When air is heated, the particles of air move farther apart, and the air becomes less dense. This lowers the air pressure because there are fewer air particles over a certain part of the earth. This is called a **low pressure** area. Water vapor also lowers air pressure because water vapor is a gas and is not as dense as air.

Cool air is more dense than warm air. It forms a **high pressure** area.

- Complete the puzzle.
  1. Air pressure is the _____ of air on the earth's surface.
  2. Water _____ lowers air pressure.
  3. Warm air _____ air pressure.
  4. Air in the earth's _____ pushes down on the earth's surface.
  5. Cool air forms _____ pressure areas.

High pressure and low pressure areas are usually located on a weather map with the symbols **H** and **L.** Cut out the weather map in the newspaper. Copy it on this map.

Fun Fact

High pressure areas on a weather map usually mean fair weather. Low pressure areas often bring changing weather.

Where the Action Is

Name _____

"Relief from this hot weather is on its way. During the night, a cold front will move into our area." Changes in the weather take place at a front. A **front** is where two air masses meet.

A **cold front** is formed when a cold air mass moves into a warm air mass. A cold front pushes the warm air up and forms dark, towering clouds. These clouds form thunderstorms that often bring brief, heavy showers.

A **warm front** forces warm air over the cool air. Warm fronts form high, thin clouds that often bring light, steady rain that may last for a day or more.

Cold fronts usually travel faster than warm fronts. When a cold front catches up to a warm front, it forms an **occluded front.**

When a front shows little or no movement, it is called a **stationary front.**

Complete the puzzle.

Across
2. Heavy rain showers with lightning.
4. Cold fronts move_____
   than warm fronts.
6. A front that doesn't move.
8. Front that forms thunderstorms.

Down
1. Two air masses meeting.
3. Warm fronts bring light,
   steady_____.
5. A front that rises over a cold air mass.
7. Cold front catches up to a warm
   front.

Challenge

Weather Map Symbols

| warm front | cold front | stationary front | occluded front |

Cut out the weather map from the newspaper or sketch the weather map from the television. Label the fronts.

IF8759 Science Enrichment

Blowing in the Wind

Name _____

Do the winds in your area seem to blow from the same direction everyday? The most common wind in your area is called the **prevailing wind.**

Weather records sometimes show the prevailing winds with a wind rose. A **wind rose** is made of a dot with a set of lines, looking like the spokes on a wheel. The length of each line shows the speed of the wind. The position of the line indicates the direction from which the wind blows.

Look carefully at the wind rose at the right. From what direction does the strongest wind usually blow? If you said the northwest, you are correct. Wind roses can be very helpful when trying to predict the direction that pollution such as smog, smoke, and noise will move in your area.

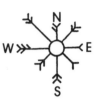

Look at the map below. Pretend that you are a city developer. Considering smog, noise, and smells, where would you locate the listed structures in your town? Draw the symbols for each structure on the map and give your reason.

[map showing compass rose, I-1, US-6, Main Street]

shopping center _____

housing development _____

airport _____

landfill (dump) _____

smoky, noisy factory _____

clean, noisy factory _____

clean, quiet factory _____

park _____

Gentle Breeze

Name _____

"Today the wind will be a gentle breeze from the northwest." The direction of a wind is always named for the direction from which the wind blows. Meteorologists use a weather vane to find the wind direction. The arrow points into the wind. What direction is the wind in the picture coming from?

_____

Wind speed can be described in many ways. It can be described with words like "gentle breeze," "strong wind," or "calm." Other times it can be given in kilometers or miles per hour as measured with an anemometer. The Beaufort Scale shown on this page is often used to describe wind speed.

1. Keep a record of the wind for this week. Write the Beaufort number and symbol.

MON.	TUE.	WED.	THUR.	FRI.

2. On a weather map, the wind symbol gives both the direction and speed. Write the direction and type of wind for these cities.

City	Wind Direction	Type of Wind
Miami		
Chicago		
Denver		
L.A.		
Seattle		
Toronto		

Beaufort Wind Scale

Number and Symbol	Description	Type of Wind	Wind Speed km/h
⊙	smoke rises straight up	calm	0-1
1	smoke drifts	light air	1-5
2	wind felt on face, leaves rustle	light breeze	6-12
3	flag blows straight out	gentle breeze	13-18
4	loose papers blow	moderate breeze	19-28
5	small trees sway	fresh breeze	29-38
6	hats blow off, branches move	strong breeze	39-50
7	difficult to walk against wind	moderate gale	51-61
8	small branches break off trees	fresh gale	62-74
9	damage to buildings	strong gale	75-87
10	trees uprooted	whole gale	88-101

IF8759 Science Enrichment

Hot and Sticky

Name _____

"Our hot, sticky weather will continue today with a relative humidity of 83%." **Relative humidity** is the amount of water vapor that the air can hold at a certain temperature. A relative humidity of 90% is very humid and uncomfortable.

Relative humidity is measured with a **hygrometer,** which is made of wet bulb and dry bulb thermometers. If the humidity is low, the water on the wet bulb thermometer will evaporate and cool the thermometer. By finding the difference between the temperatures on both thermometers and using a chart, you can find the relative humidity.

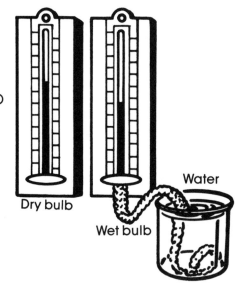

Dry bulb

Wet bulb

Water

1. Michelle recorded the following data over a period of one week. Use the table to find the relative humidity.

Day	Dry Temp.	Wet Temp.	Difference	Relative Humidity
Mon.	21°	20°		
Tue.	23°	21°		
Wed.	22°	20°		
Thur.	21°	17°		
Fri.	21°	16°		
Sat.	20°	16°		
Sun.	20°	17°		

Table

Dry bulb temp. °C	Difference between wet and dry temperatures							
	1°	2°	3°	4°	5°	6°	7°	8°
15°	90	80	71	61	53	44	36	27
16°	90	81	71	63	54	46	38	30
17°	90	81	72	64	55	47	40	32
18°	91	82	73	65	57	49	41	34
19°	91	82	74	65	58	50	43	36
20°	91	83	74	66	59	51	44	37
21°	91	83	75	67	60	53	46	39
22°	92	83	76	68	61	54	47	40
23°	92	84	76	69	62	55	48	42
24°	92	84	77	69	62	56	49	43
25°	92	84	77	70	63	57	50	44
26°	92	85	78	71	64	58	51	46
27°	92	85	78	71	65	58	52	47

2. Use Michelle's data to make a graph of the relative humidity.

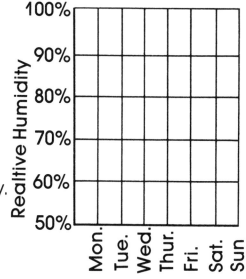

Rain, Snow, Sleet, and Hail

Name _____

Neither rain, snow, sleet, nor hail will stop the dedicated postmen and postwomen. They will not be stopped by any form of precipitation. **Precipitation** is water vapor that condenses and falls to the earth.

All precipitation starts as water vapor. The water vapor cools and then condenses, forming water droplets or ice crystals, depending on the temperature. The form of the precipitation depends on the temperature, air currents, and the humidity.

• Identify each form of precipitation with the correct symbol.

☰	⸴	●	⩒	✳	△	⧨
fog	drizzle	rain	heavy rain	snow	sleet	hail

1.	light mist of droplets falling to the earth	4.	vapor that changes directly into a solid because of freezing temperatures	7.	droplets that freeze and are bounced up and down through the cloud, building layers
2.	droplets that freeze as they get closer to the ground	5.	water vapor that forms droplets and falls to the earth		
3.	large amount of droplets falling to the earth	6.	clouds that form close to the ground		

• Record the precipitation twice each day this week using the correct symbols.

AM	PM	AM	PM	AM	PM	AM	PM	AM	PM	AM	PM	AM	PM
Sunday		Monday		Tuesday		Wednesday		Thursday		Friday		Saturday	

Fun Fact
The wettest place in the world is on the island of Maui in Hawaii. It rains 350 days of the year!

Partly Cloudy

Name _____

"This morning the skies will be clear with clouds forming in the early afternoon." **Clouds** are formed when a rising mass of air is cooled. Rising warm air reaches levels where the air pressure is lower, causing the air to expand. As air expands, it uses up heat energy, and the air becomes colder. If the air is cooled below the dew point, the water vapor in the air condenses as tiny droplets or ice crystals and forms a cloud.

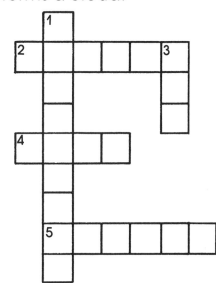

1. Water vapor _____ to form water droplets.

2. Warm, moist air condenses when it is

   _____.

3. Water vapor forms droplets when it is cooled

   below the _____ point.

4. Expanding air uses up _____ energy.

5. Lower air pressure causes the warm air to

   _____.

Meteorologists use shaded circle symbols to record the amount of cloud cover in the sky. The location of the clouds in the sky can also be shown by shading the matching part of the circle.

1/4 cover in the southeast

completely overcast

3/4 covered

1/2 covered

1/4 covered

scattered clouds

no clouds

● Record the cloud cover for one week using the symbols above.

Sunday	Monday	Tuesday	Wednesday	Thursday	Friday	Saturday
◯	◯	◯	◯	◯	◯	◯

IF8759 Science Enrichment

Cloudy Weather

Name _____

There are three basic types of clouds.

Cirrus — High, thin, feathery clouds. They often mean good weather.

Stratus — Low clouds that form layers. They usually mean stormy weather.

Cumulus — Puffy clouds that form in heaps. They usually mean fair weather.

Two other words help describe the three basic types of clouds.

Nimbus or **nimbo** means rain.

Alto means forming in the middle layer in the sky.

Most clouds are a combination of the three basic types of clouds. The cloud types and their symbols are listed below.

High Clouds	Middle Clouds	Low Clouds	Clouds found at all heights
Cirrus ⌒ Cirrocumulus ⌇ Cirrostratus ⌒	Altocumulus ⌣ Altostratus ∠	Stratocumulus ⌣ Stratus — Nimbostratus ⫽	Cumulus ⌓ Cumulonimbus ⌼

- Use the chart, symbols, and descriptions of the three basic types of clouds to identify the clouds described below.

1. high, thin, bumpy clouds _____

2. low, gray rain clouds _____

3. puffy rain clouds _____

4. high, thin, layered clouds _____

- Record the types of clouds and describe the weather for one week.

Cloud Type							
Weather							
	Sun.	Mon.	Tues.	Wed.	Thur.	Fri.	Sat.

 IF8759 Science Enrichment

Br-r-r-r

Name _____

On a hot summer day, one of the most comfortable places to be is sitting in front of a fan. Why does this make you feel cooler? The air the fan is blowing is the same temperature as the air in the rest of the room. But the wind from the fan evaporates your perspiration, which lowers the temperature of your skin.

Outside, the wind can have the same cooling effect. This is called **wind chill.** Wind chill is found on a wind chill chart using the temperature and the wind speed.

1. Ryan collected the following data. Find the wind chill.

Day	Wind Speed	Temp.	Wind Chill
Sun.	8 km/hr	10°	_____
Mon.	32 km/hr	− 1°	_____
Tues.	24 km/hr	4°	_____
Wed.	calm	− 1°	_____
Thur.	8 km/hr	− 17°	_____
Fri.	16 km/hr	− 6°	_____
Sat.	40 km/hr	− 12°	_____

Wind Chill Chart
Thermometer Reading °C

Wind Speed (km/hr)	10°	4°	−1°	−6°	−12°	−17°	−23°
calm	10°	4°	−1°	−6°	−12°	−17°	−23°
8	8°	2°	−2°	−8°	−14°	−20°	−26°
16	4°	−2°	−8°	−15°	−22°	−29°	−36°
24	2°	−5°	−12°	−20°	−27°	−38°	−43°
32	0°	−7°	−15°	−23°	−32°	−39°	−46°
40	−1°	−8°	−17°	−26°	−34°	−42°	−50°
48	−2°	−10°	−18°	−27°	−36°	−44°	−58°
56	−2.5°	−11°	−20°	−28°	−37°	−45°	−58°
64	−3°	−12°	−21°	−29°	−39°	−48°	−56°

2. Chart Ryan's data on the graph at the right. Use one line to show the actual temperature and another to show wind chill.

3. Which two days have the same actual temperature?

_____

Why are the wind chill temperatures

different? _____

4. Which day has the largest difference between wind chill and actual temperature?

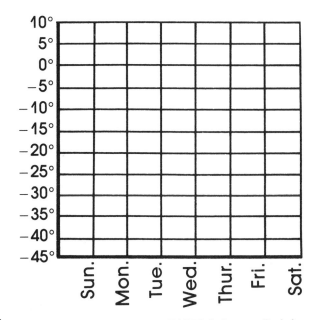

Thunderboomers

Name _____

Flash-boom! Two things must happen in order for a **thunderstorm** to form. First, warm air must rise quickly, causing an **updraft**. Second, the updraft must contain large amounts of water vapor.

As the warm, moist air quickly rises, it cools and condenses into tiny droplets or ice crystals. As a result, a cloud forms. The condensing water vapor warms the air and causes the cloud to build higher and higher, forming a **thunderhead.**

Each water droplet carries a tiny electrical charge. With each thunderhead containing billions of droplets, the electrical charge builds up. Electricity jumps from the top of the cloud to the bottom, causing a giant spark called **lightning.** The lightning heats the air, causing it to **expand** rapidly. The rapidly expanding air causes vibrations called **thunder.**

1. Number the steps in order for the formation of a thunderstorm.

    _____ a thunderhead forms

    _____ warm air quickly rises

    _____ a cloud forms

    _____ water vapor cools and condenses

    _____ cloud builds higher and higher

2. Put a ✔ in front of each precaution you should take during a thunderstorm.

    _____ remain indoors

    _____ stand under a tree

    _____ stay away from metal fences

    _____ swim in lakes but not swimming pools

    _____ carry an umbrella on the golf course

    _____ stay away from the television and telephone

Fun Fact

There is enough electricity in one flash of lightning to light your house for a whole year.

FLASH-BOOM!

Name _____

FLASH — a bolt of lightning brightens the sky. You slowly count to 15 and then — **BOOM** — thunder! With this information, you are able to estimate how far the storm is from you.

Lightning and thunder occur at approximately the same time, but you see the lightning before you hear the thunder. That is because light travels much faster than sound. On a typical, warm summer day, sound travels one kilometer in three seconds. How far away is the storm if you count 15 seconds? Follow these steps to find out.

1. Time the FLASH to BOOM in seconds. _15 sec._____

2. Divide the seconds by 3. (3 km/sec)

3. Your answer is in kilometers._____

$$\frac{5}{3\overline{)15}}$$
$$\frac{15}{0}$$

(If your answer has a remainder, you may round off to the nearest whole number.)

Matt timed eight FLASH-BOOMS in a storm as it approached and passed. Using Matt's data, find the distance of the storm with each passing FLASH-BOOM. Circle the time and distance when the storm was the closest.

	Time	Distance
1.	63 sec.	____ km
2.	48 sec.	
3.	24 sec.	
4.	18 sec.	

	Time	Distance
5.	9 sec.	
6.	3 sec.	
7.	12 sec.	
8.	27 sec.	

What does it mean if you see a flash and hear a boom at the same time?

_____

What factors can make our estimation of the distance of the lightning

less accurate?_____

_____

Fun Fact

A beam of light travels from the moon to the earth in less than two seconds. It takes almost two weeks for sound to travel the same distance.

Whirlpools of Wind

Name _____

The spinning winds of a twisting funnel cloud, called a **tornado,** are the most violent winds on Earth. These winds can be as strong as 500 km/hr and travel in a path a few hundred meters wide. Air pressure is so low in the center of the tornado that objects which are in the funnel's path, like houses, explode from the expanding air trapped inside.

No one knows exactly what causes tornadoes. One theory is that a front of moving, cool, dry air overruns warm, moist air. The warm, moist air is trapped below and rushes upwards. More warm air rushes in from the sides and causes warm updrafts to twist and spin. Tornadoes last only a short time, but if they touch the ground they can cause horrible destruction.

To keep us safe during a tornado, the National Weather Bureau issues **tornado warnings** and **tornado watches.**

1. What is a tornado watch? _____

2. What is a tornado warning? _____

3. What should you do if you are at home when a tornado warning is issued?

_____

at school? _____

walking in your neighborhood? _____

● Solve these tornado twisters.

1. Tornadoes are called _____ clouds.

2. The explanation of a tornado's origin is only a _____.

3. The _____ _____ in the center of a tornado is very low.

4. Objects _____ in a tornado.

Fun Fact

In 1973, a tornado in France crossed a pond, sucking everything into the air. A few miles away, there was a surprise "rainfall" of water, fish, and frogs as the tornado dropped its load.

    98   IF8759 Science Enrichment

Willy-Willies

Name _____

Over warm oceans in areas near the equator, the world's most powerful storms are formed. These large, rotating masses of warm, moist air, called **hurricanes,** bring heavy rains and very strong winds.

Hurricanes form when cool, light winds aloft combine with the warm, moist ocean air. This warm, moist air spirals upwards, releasing heat and causing the winds to grow stronger. The winds can reach a speed of 350 km/hr and measure over 650 km wide. The **eye,** or center of the hurricane, may be very calm. Hurricanes move slowly and last for a number of days. The high winds and heavy rains of a hurricane can cause great damage.

Hurricanes are called **willy-willies** in Australia, **typhoons** in the North Atlantic, **cyclones** in the Indian Ocean, and **baguios** in the Philippine Sea.

Use the information from this page and other sources to compare the characteristics of tornadoes and hurricanes. Place an **X** in the correct column.

	Tornado	Hurricane
1. Causes much damage to property.		
2. Has very high winds.		
3. Travels a path that is less than a mile wide.		
4. Associated with storms near the equator.		
5. Warnings give as much as two days' notice.		
6. Given "names" by the National Weather Service.		
7. Very calm in the center.		
8. Low air pressure causes objects to explode in its center.		
9. Lasts only a few minutes.		
10. Causes high ocean tides and waves.		

Find Out

Hurricanes are given names. How does the National Weather Service decide on the name? What are the names of some of the most destructive hurricanes in the past 30 years?

Mapping the Weather

Name _____

Weather maps show the recorded weather conditions over a large area. These maps are usually made by the computers of the National Weather Service. They are used to help predict weather changes.

There are many types of weather maps. The one on this page is typical of those found in many newspapers. It gives air pressure in units called **millibars,** written at the end of each isobar.

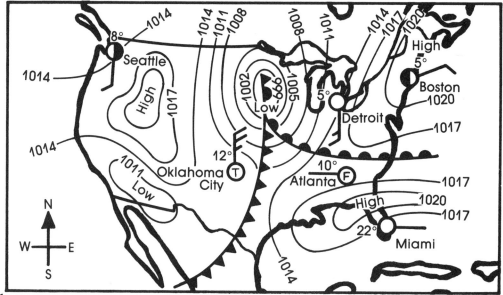

Cold front	◐ Partly cloudy	Temperature (°C)		
Warm front	Ⓢ Snow	West Wind	Direction of wind	East Wind
Occluded front	Ⓕ Fog		Wind velocity (km/h)	
○ Clear	Hurricane	○ 0-1 ○ 13-18 ○ 39-50 ○ 75-87		
Ⓡ Rain	● Cloudy	○ 1-5 ○ 19-28 ○ 51-61 ○ 88-101		
Ⓣ Thunderstorm	Ⓩ Freezing rain	○ 6-12 ○ 29-38 ○ 62-74		

1. What is the temperature in Seattle?_____

2. What is the direction of the wind in Miami?_____

3. What city has fog?_____

4. What kind of front is east of Oklahoma City?_____

5. What kind of front is north of Atlanta?_____

6. What kind of front was formed where the cold front met the warm front?

_____

7. What kind of cloud cover is found in Miami?_____

8. What is the cloud cover like in Boston?_____

9. What is the barometric pressure in millibars for the city of Seattle?_____

Something Special

If you would like accurate weather maps of your own, contact the meteorologists at the nearest large radio or T.V. station.

"Red Sky at Night"

Name _____

"Will Saturday be a good day to go the beach?" Better look at the weather forecast. The National Weather Service makes short range forecasts (up to three days) using basic weather instruments, information from weather maps, and records of past weather patterns.

- Use the information from the chart to make weather predictions for the situations below.

Wind Direction	Sea-Level Barometric Pressure (mm)	Weather to be Expected
SW to NW	764.54 to 767.08, steady	Fair, with little temperature change for 1-2 days.
SW to NW	764.58 to 767.08, rising fast	Fair, followed by rain within 2 days.
SW to NW	767.08 and above, steady	Continued fair, no marked temperature change.
S to E	756.92 or below, falling fast	Severe storm, followed within 24 hours by clearing and, in winter, colder temperatures.
S to SW	762.00 or below, rising slowly	Clearing within a few hours, fair for several days.
Going to W	745.00 or below, rising fast	Clearing and colder.
E to N	756.92 or below, falling fast	Severe NE gale and heavy rain. In winter, heavy snow and cold wave.
SE to NE	762.00 or below, falling slowly	Steady rain for 1-2 days.
SE to NE	762.00 or below, falling fast	Rain, high wind, clearing in 36 hours and cooler.
S to SE	764.58 to 767.08, falling slowly	Rain within 24 hours.

Data

1. Southwest wind, barometric pressure 767.20mm, steady _____

    _____

2. South wind, barometric pressure 765.00, falling slowly _____

    _____

3. South wind, barometric pressure 756.00, falling fast _____

    _____

4. Southeast wind, barometric pressure 761.51, falling slowly _____

    _____

5. Southwest wind, barometric pressure 765.10, steady _____

    _____

6. What kind of weather usually comes with rising barometric pressure?

    _____

7. What kind of weather usually comes with falling barometric pressure?

    _____

Find Out

Weather Proverbs: Ask your parents about weather proverbs in your area such as, "Red sky at night, sailors delight. Red sky in morn', sailors forewarn."

Weather Tools

Name _____

Meteorologists use many basic instruments to gather their data. You may already have many of these instruments in your home. If not, you can construct them from easy-to-find materials. Many fine books are available that show you how to construct your own weather station.

Modern forecasting also relies on many sophisticated electronic instruments. Radar is used to track areas of precipitation hundreds of miles away. Pictures of cloud formations from all over the world are available from weather-tracking satellites.

• Solve the puzzle using both the picture clues and the written clues.

Down
1. Cloud direction indicator.
2. Precipitation is measured with a rain _____.
3. Measures air pressure.
4. A weather _____ shows wind direction.

Across
5. Measures relative humidity.
6. Measures wind speed.
7. Measures temperature.

Word Bank

anemometer   nephoscope
barometer   thermometer
gauge   vane
hygrometer

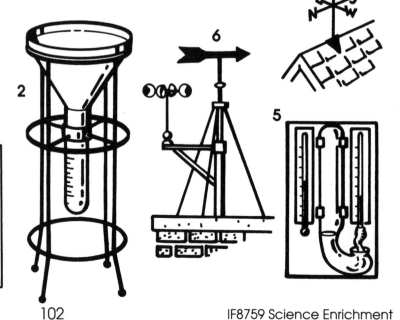

Answer Key

Plant Parts

Name _____

Whether you live in the warm Florida Everglades, the mountains of British Columbia, or someplace in between, you live in a world of green, flowering plants. Look at the plants that grow near you. Can you name the plants' parts? Green, flowering plants have six basic parts: root, stem, flower, fruit, leaf, and seed.

Label the parts of the bean plant using the words from the word bank.

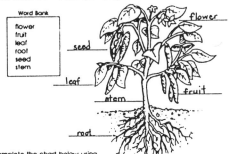

Word Bank

flower
fruit
leaf
root
seed
stem

Complete the chart below using words from the word bank.

Plant Part	Function
seed	grows into a new plant
fruit	holds and protects the seeds
stem	carries water from the roots to the leaves and food from the leaves to the roots
root	holds the plant in the soil and collects water and minerals from the soil
leaf	makes food for the plant
flower	makes new seeds through reproduction

What's Blooming?

Name _____

Flowers vary greatly in size, color, and shape. The blossoms of grass are so tiny that we rarely see them, while the flower of the chrysanthemum is large and beautiful. But all flowers have basically the same parts and the same important function–to produce seeds.

Look carefully at the picture of the apple blossom. Notice the five parts. The tulip and the lily are very similar. Label the five parts of the lily and the tulip using words from the word bank. Then complete the chart.

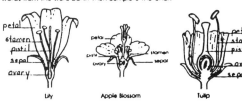

Lily   Apple Blossom   Tulip

Word Bank

ovary
petal
pistil
sepal
stamen

Flower Part	Description
sepal	small leaf-like structure at the base of the flower
petals	attractive leaves that are often colorful and sweetly scented
ovary	boat-shaped structure where the seeds develop
pistil	large center stalk, often shaped like a water bottle
stamen	slender stalks with knobbed tips holding grains of pollen

Something Special

Florists usually throw away flowers that are beginning to look wilted and unattractive. Ask a florist for any flowers that are ready to be thrown away. Take the flowers apart and try to identify the parts.

More Flowers

Name _____

Flowers have the important function of producing seeds. The male part of a flower is called the stamen. At the tip of the stamen is the anther, a tiny case with many grains of pollen. The female part of a flower is called the pistil. The tip of the pistil is the stigma, the long neck is the style, and the large base is the ovary. The ovary holds the tiny ovules, which develop into seeds.

Label the parts of the flower using the words in bold from above.

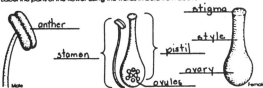

Complete each sentence with the missing word.

1. The anther is filled with p o l l e n
2. The stigma is held up by the s t y l e
3. The female flower part is the p i s t i l
4. Seeds form in the o v a r y
5. Seeds develop from tiny o v u l e s
6. The tip of the pistil is the s t i g m a
7. The male flower part is the s t a m e n

Something Special

Use the numbered letters to answer the riddle.

"If April showers bring May flowers, what do May flowers bring?"

P i l g r i m s
1 2 3 4 5 6 7 8

Gold Dust

Name _____

Golden grains of pollen are encased in the anther on the top of the stamen. When these golden grains touch the stigma, a long pollen tube grows down to the ovary. The pollen cells meet with the ovule to form a seed. This process is called fertilization.

Some flowers have both male and female parts. These plants can fertilize themselves. However, the pollen usually comes from another flower. The pollen grains travel in the wind, by insects, or by birds. Why do you think many fruit growers keep beehives in their orchards?

Study the pictures below. Tell how each flower is being pollinated.

The pollen is being carried by the wind.

The pollen sticks to the bird as it flies from flower to flower.

Number the following sentences in the proper order.

2 Pollen grains fall on the stigma.

1 Pollen forms on the stamen.

5 The ovule and pollen form a seed.

3 A pollen tube grows down to the ovary.

4 Pollen cells meet with the ovule.

Find Out

Bees store pollen in waxed cells in the hive. This stored pollen, called "bee bread," is used to feed baby bees. How do bees carry pollen?

Answer Key

Anchors Away!

Name _____

Have you ever tried to pull a large plant out of the ground? Sometimes it can be quite a struggle. That's because roots are holding it in place.

Roots do more than hold a plant in the ground. They also collect water and minerals for the plant.

There are two kinds of root systems. Some plants have shallow roots with many branches. These are called fibrous roots. The other root system has only one main root that digs deep into the ground. This is called the tap root.

Water gathering is not done by large, thick roots; thick roots have a waterproof, outside layer. Instead, hundreds of small, fine roots, called root hairs, have the job of collecting water and minerals.

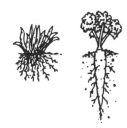

fibrous root   tap root

Label the type of root system. Also label the root hairs.

It has been a long, dry, hot summer. Mr. Williams' grass is turning brown, but the dandelions are bright green.
1. What kind of root system does his grass have? __fibrous root__
2. What kind of root system do his dandelions have? __tap root__
3. Why does the dandelion stay green while the grass turns brown? __The dandelion's tap root can go down deep to where the soil is still moist.__
4. Draw the root systems for the grass and dandelions.

Fun Facts

The tap root of an alfalfa plant can grow as much as four meters deep in one season!

Food Factories

Name _____

Leaves are like little factories designed to do an important job–make food. Different parts of the leaf help with this job. The veins in a leaf are bundles of tiny tubes. They carry water and minerals to the leaf and take food from the leaf to the rest of the plant. Veins also help hold the leaf up.

On the underside of the leaf are small openings called stomata. Stomata have been called the lungs of a leaf because they allow air to enter the leaf.

The outer layers of the leaf are covered with a waxy layer which prevents the leaf from drying out.

Why are leaves green? Leaf cells contain small particles called chloroplasts. Each chloroplast contains a complex, green material called chlorophyll which gives the leaf its color.

Label the parts of the leaf using words from the word bank.

Word Bank
veins
stomata
waxy layer

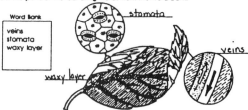

stomata
veins
waxy layer

Complete the puzzle using the words in bold

Across
2. Bundles of tiny tubes that carry water, minerals, and food
4. Openings in a leaf allow _____ to enter.
5. Substance that gives a leaf its green color

Down
1. Surface of a leaf feels _____.
3. Small openings on the underside of the leaf

Crossword answers: veins, air, chlorophyll, stomata

Food from the Sun

Name _____

With the help of chlorophyll and energy from the sun, a leaf can change lifeless substances into food. This process is called photosynthesis.

Plants need water (H_2O) and carbon dioxide (CO_2) to make food by photosynthesis. The water is gathered by the plant's roots. Carbon dioxide, found in the air, is gathered through tiny openings, called stomata, located on the underside of the leaf.

The leaf uses chlorophyll and sunlight to change water and carbon dioxide into oxygen and sugar. The sugar is mixed with water and sent to other parts of the plant. Oxygen is released into the air through the stomata.

Complete the formula for photosynthesis using the words in bold above.

Photosynthesis = __water__ + __carbon dioxide__ + __chlorophyll__ + __sunlight__

Scott's dad gave him some healthy houseplants. Scott decided to keep them in his room, but his room was always dark. What do you think will happen to Scott's plants? Why?
__Scott's plants may become weak and die because there is no sunlight for photosynthesis to take place.__

Sarah set up her aquarium with some fish and aquatic plants. Explain how the fish and the plants benefit from each other.
__The fish breathes in oxygen and breathe out carbon dioxide. The plants take in carbon dioxide and release oxygen.__

Find Out

To make one-half kg of sugar, a plant must breathe over one million liters of air. What kind of plants produce the sugar that is in the sugar bowl in your kitchen?

Plant Pipelines

Name _____

How does the plant get its food? Thin tubes in the stem carry food from the leaf to the rest of the plant. Other tubes carry water and minerals from the roots to the leaves. Both kinds of tubes are found in bundles in the stem.

The tube bundles are arranged in two ways. A monocot stem has bundles scattered throughout the stem. Dicot stems have their bundles arranged in a ring around the edge of the stem.

monocot   dicot

Dicot or monocot stem? Label the two pictures above.

Experiment: Observing Plant Pipelines
Materials:
drinking glass
water
food coloring
eye dropper
knife
stalk of celery

Directions:
Put a few drops of food coloring in a glass of water. Trim off the bottom 2 cm of a stalk of celery. Place the celery in the water. Let stand for 3-4 hours.

Results:
1. Describe what you see. __Colored water rises up the stem of the celery.__
2. Cut the stalk crosswise. Look at the cut ends. What do you see? __bundles of thin tubes__
3. What carried the water up the stalk? __tube bundles__
4. What would happen if the stem of a plant were broken? Why? __Food and water would not reach the leaves. The plant would die because the leaves need water for photosynthesis.__

Something Special

Try the experiment above, but with a new twist. Use a white flower instead of celery; carnations or daisies work great. Watch what happens!

Answer Key

Tree History

Name _____

A freshly cut tree stump can be read like a tree's own personal diary. By looking closely at the rings, called annual rings, you can interpret clues that tell you about the tree's life.

Each ring in a tree represents one year of growth. Wide light rings usually indicate that the tree had a good growing season. Rings that are close together indicate years of slow growth. Scars and cuts may mean that the tree was in a fire or struck by lightning.

The tree pictured on this page was cut just last week. How much can you learn about its life?

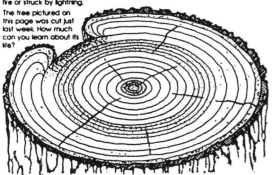

1. How old is this tree? __18 years__
2. What year was it planted? __Present year – 18 years = answer__
3. With a blue pencil or crayon, color the ring of the year you were born.
4. Color the rings of the slow growing years red.
5. What could have caused this slow growth? __no rain__

6. What could have caused the large scar on the tree? __1) a forest fire,__
   __2) someone could have chopped some of the bark off__
   __the tree__

Monocot or Dicot?

Name _____

Flowering plants are divided into two main groups–the dicots, or dicotyledons, and the monocots, or monocotyledons. The basic differences can be found by looking at their seeds. The dicots have two cotyledons, or food parts, and the monocots have one cotyledon, or food part.

There are other differences in their leaves, stems, and flowers. The differences are noted in the chart below.

Plant Part	Monocot	Dicot
leaves	The veins are parallel	The veins form a net-like structure
stem	The bundles of tubes are scattered throughout the stem.	The bundles of tubes form a ring around the outside of the stem.
flower	The petals and stamen are in groups of three, six, and nine.	The petal and stamen are in groups of four and five
seeds	The seeds have one cotyledon or food part.	The seeds have two cotyledons or food parts.

Identify each of the plant parts below as a dicot or monocot.

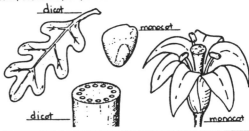

Something Special

Find some common plants around your home or school and classify them as monocot or dicot.

Cone-Bearing Plants

Name _____

Plants, like pine trees, that develop seeds in cones are called conifers. Conifers have two kinds of cones. The smaller male cone develops pollen grains. Egg cells develop in the ovule of the much larger female cone. Pollen from the male cone is carried by the wind and lodges in the scales of the female cone. A pollen tube grows down to the ovule, and a new seed is formed. After the seeds are ripe, the cone and the seed drop to the ground.

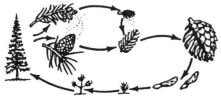

1. In what way is seed formation in a conifer the same as in a flowering plant? __The pollen grows to the ovule, and a new seed is formed.__

2. How is seed formation in a conifer different than in a flowering plant? __Conifers do not have flowers. They have male and female cones. Most flowers have both the male and female parts in the same flower.__

Number the following steps in the correct order.

__4__ A seed is formed.

__6__ A new conifer sprouts from the seed.

__1__ Pollen grains are carried by the wind.

__3__ A pollen tube grows down to the ovule.

__2__ Pollen grains lodge in the scales of the female cone.

__5__ Ripened seeds are released from the cone.

Fun Facts

The giant redwood trees are unquestionably the world's tallest trees. The largest of these conifers, found in Humboldt County, California, has been measured at over 100 meters tall.

Fiddleheads to Ferns

Name _____

Have you ever seen little green "fiddleheads" growing out of the moist soil? These will soon be beautiful ferns. Ferns, like flowering green plants, have roots, stems, and leaves. But they do not make seeds. Ferns reproduce from spores. Most ferns are about 25 cm tall, but some are as small as 2 cm or as tall as trees!

Tiny brown dots, containing hundreds of spores, line the underside of the fern leaf. Spores that fall on a wet place grow into tiny heart-shaped plants. Each tiny plant produces both the sperm and the egg cells. After a rain, the sperm cell will swim to the egg cell through the water. When the sperm fertilizes an egg cell, a new young fern will grow. Making food by photosynthesis, the young fiddlehead will grow into a mature fern plant.

Complete the chart using information from above.

Plant parts	roots, stems, leaves
How the fern makes food	photosynthesis
Size of plant	2 cm to tree size - most around 25 cm
Method of reproducing	reproduce from spores

1. Why must ferns live in wet places? __To reproduce, the sperm cell must be able to swim to the egg cell.__

2. How are ferns like flowering plants? __They both have roots, stems, and leaves, and they make food by photosynthesis.__

3. How are ferns different than flowering plants? __Ferns do not make seeds but reproduce with spores.__

Find Out

Millions of years ago, the earth was covered with ferns. Today, there is still evidence of these giant plants. The products of these plants are extremely valuable to man. Can you name the products? How were they formed?

Nature's Green Carpet

Name _____

Have you ever seen a smooth, green, velvety carpet growing on a moist forest floor? This carpet is made of hundreds of tiny moss plants growing closely together.

Mosses, like ferns, do not produce seeds; they reproduce with spores. Sperm cells and egg cells are formed at the top of the moss plant. After a rain, the sperm travels through the water to the egg cell. The fertilized egg cell sprouts a tall stalk with a case for the spores at its tip. These spores will produce new mosses. Mosses make their food by photosynthesis, but unlike other green plants, they do not have roots, leaves, or stems. Mosses are small and grow only a few centimeters high. Food and water travel slowly from cell to cell.

Complete the chart using the information from above.

Plant parts	spores, cells
How it gets its food	photosynthesis
Size	a few centimeters
Method of reproducing	spores

1. Why must mosses live in wet places? 1) for the sperm cell to travel in water for reproduction, 2) They do not have roots to gather water.

2. How are mosses like ferns? Both reproduce with spores.

3. How are mosses different from other green plants? Mosses do not have roots, leaves, or stems.

Find Out

An old woodsman's survival tip says, "Moss usually grows on the north side of a tree." Why is this usually true?

Fungus Among Us

Name _____

"Yuch! This bread has green fuzz on it!" The fuzz is mold. Mold and mushrooms are fungi.

A fungus plant is not a true plant, because it does not have roots, stems, leaves, or chlorophyll. Fungi cannot make their own food like green plants. Instead, they get their energy by absorbing food from dead or living matter.

Most fungi reproduce by forming spores. The spores fall on dead organisms. A tiny cell breaks out of the spore and grows into fuzzy threads. The threads form new caps, stalks, or capsules.

Fungi are helpful members of nature's recycling team. They help break down dead organisms that can then become part of the soil.

Complete the following sentences using the words in bold.

1. Most fungi reproduce by forming s p o r e s.
2. Fungi do not have roots, s t e m s, or l e a v e s.
3. Fungi cannot make their own f o o d.
4. Fungi are not green, they lack c h l o r o p h y l l.
5. Mold and mushrooms are f u n g i.
6. Fungi break down dead organisms that then become part of the s o i l.

Use the numbered letters to solve the riddle.

"What kind of room has no walls, windows, or doors?"

m u s h r o o m

Find Out

Get an unwashed mushroom from a store. Cut off the mushroom cap. Place the cap, gill side down, on a sheet of paper. Place a bowl over the cap. Let it set for one day. Remove the bowl and mushroom cap. Presto! It's a print. What is that dust that formed the print?

Baker's Buddy

Name _____

Yeast is another kind of fungus. Yeast differs from other fungi in two ways. First, yeast is made of only one cell. Second, yeast can reproduce in two ways. Each cell can grow a small bump, called a bud. When this bud grows large enough, it breaks off and forms a new cell. This is called budding. The second way of reproducing is when the cell divides two or three times inside the cell case. The new cells become spores and stay inside until the case breaks open.

Yeast grows rapidly when it has sugar for food. When yeast breaks down the sugar, it gives off carbon dioxide gas bubbles and alcohol. These bubbles cause bread dough to swell up. Yeast really is a baker's buddy!

Answer the following questions by unscrambling the letters in each yeast cell. The letters will "bud" into the correct answers.

1. Yeast is a kind of fungus — fungus
2. Yeast is made of only one cell — cell
3. Reproducing by making little bumps is called budding — budding
4. Yeast divides in the cell case and forms spores — spores
5. Yeast feeds on sugar — sugar
6. Yeast produces bubbles of gas — gas

Find Out

Find out what Matza is. How does it get its name?

Algae

Name _____

Algae can be found growing on the sides of your aquarium, in puddles in your yard, as seaweed in the ocean, or almost any place where there is water.

Algae is one of the simplest forms of plant life. Like fungus, algae does not have roots, stems, or leaves. Unlike fungus, algae has chlorophyll and can make its own food by photosynthesis.

Algae can range in size from single cells to the giant Pacific kelp that grows to a length of sixty centimeters!

1. In what ways is algae similar to fungi? It does not have roots, stems, or leaves.

2. In what way is algae different than fungi? It has chlorophyll and can make its own food by photosynthesis.

Complete the chart using the information from above.

Size	single cell to 60 centimeters
How it makes food	photosynthesis
Habitat	almost any place there is water
Plant parts	cells

Find Out

Lichens are some of the plant world's most unusual organisms. Actually, lichens are two organisms—algae and fungi—that live together. Do some research on lichens. Why are lichens so unusual? Could algae and fungi survive alone? Explain.

IF8759 Science Enrichment

A World of Plants

Name _____

From the small, one-celled algae to the giant redwood trees, our world is filled with thousands of different kinds of plants. Scientists have a special way of classifying, or grouping, the many kinds of plants. Study the diagram below.

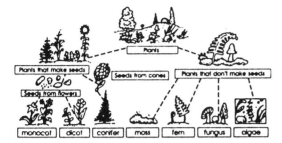

Look carefully at the plant characteristics listed below. Place a (✓) in the column or columns that represent the plant with that characteristic.

	monocot	dicot	conifer	moss	fern	fungus	algae
1. is green	✓	✓	✓	✓	✓		✓
2. makes seeds	✓	✓	✓				
3. makes seeds in a flower	✓	✓					
4. flower made seed with two seed parts		✓					
5. flower made seed with one seed part	✓						
6. makes seeds in a cone			✓				
7. produces spores				✓	✓	✓	
8. has leaves with veins	✓	✓					
9. has leaves with parallel veins	✓						
10. has leaves with net-like veins		✓					
11. has needle-like leaves			✓				
12. one-celled plant						✓	✓

Puzzling Plants

Name _____

Complete the puzzle using the words from the word bank.

Across
1. Gold dust found in the stamen
3. Makes seeds in a cone
4. Product of photosynthesis
7. Means of reproduction for ferns, molds, and yeast
8. See diagram
11. Plant's food making process
12. See diagram

Down
1. See diagram
2. See diagram
3. Green coloring in leaves
5. See diagram
6. See diagram
7. See diagram
9. See diagram
10. Two food parts

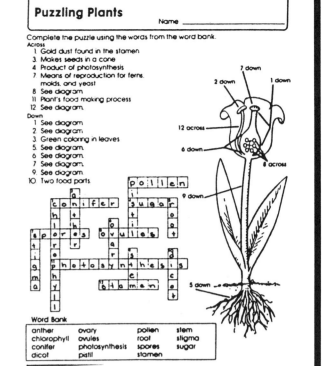

Word Bank

anther	ovary	pollen	stem
chlorophyll	ovules	root	stigma
conifer	photosynthesis	spores	sugar
dicot	pistil	stamen	

Classy Creatures

Name _____

C L A S S I F Y

Scientists use a special tool to help them find the names of insects, trees, and many other things. It is called a dichotomist key.

Each of the creatures above has a name. We will use our own dichotomist key to give each creature its name. To use the key, work with only one creature at a time. First read steps 1a and 1b. Decide which statement is true about the creature. Then follow the directions after that step. The directions will lead you to a new pair of steps. Keep this up until you come to a step that gives you the creature's name. Write the creature's name in the space provided. After you have named all of the creatures, you will be able to complete the following sentence.

A dichotomist key is used to **c l a s s i f y**

If this is true,	do this.
1 a. The creature has two eyes.	Go to step 2.
b. The creature has one eye.	Go to step 5.
2 a. The creature has one or more antennae.	Go to step 3.
b. The creature has no antennae.	Its name is "L."
3 a. The creature has one antenna.	Its name is "L."
b. The creature has more than one antenna.	Go to step 4.
4 a. The creature has two antennae.	Its name is "S."
b. The creature has three antennae.	Its name is "Y."
5 a. The creature has one or more antennae.	Go to step 6.
b. The creature has no antennae.	Its name is "A."
6 a. The creature has one antenna.	Its name is "F."
b. The creature has two antennae.	Its name is "C."

Something Special

Draw your own friendly creature from space. Give your creature from zero to three antennae and one or two eyes. Have a friend use the dichotomist key above to find what letter the creature is wearing.

Backbone or No Backbone

Name _____

The animal kingdom can be divided into two groups, vertebrates and invertebrates. Vertebrates are animals with backbones. The backbone is made of several bones called vertebrae. Each vertebra is separated by a thin disc of cartilage. The backbone supports the body and helps the animal move.

Invertebrates are animals without backbones. Have you ever looked closely at an ant or fly? They do not have a backbone or any other bones in their bodies. Some invertebrates, like crabs and lobsters, have hard, outer-body coverings. Some invertebrates, like worms, are soft all the way through their bodies.

Circle all of the hidden animals in the puzzle below. Then list them in their own group.

Word Bank

butterfly	skunk
cow	snail
crayfish	snake
deer	spider
dog	swan
fish	wasp
grasshopper	worm

Vertebrates	Invertebrates
cow	butterfly
deer	crayfish
dog	grasshopper
fish	snail
skunk	spider
snake	wasp
swan	worm

Find Out

About 1,000,000 kinds of animals have been classified by scientists. Only 45,000 are vertebrates. How many are invertebrates?

IF8759 Science Enrichment

Warm and Cold-Blooded Animals

Name _____

Mammals and birds are warm-blooded animals. Warm-blooded animals maintain a constant body temperature with the help of hair or feathers as insulation. Warm-blooded animals are called endothermic animals.

Cold-blooded animals, such as fish, reptiles, and amphibians, get their body heat from their surroundings. Their body temperature varies according to the temperature of their environment. Cold-blooded animals are called ectothermic animals.

Circle all of the animals in the wordsearch below using the words from the word bank. Then list the animals in the proper group.

Word Bank

bear	rat
deer	salamander
duck	shark
eagle	snake
fox	toad
frog	trout
lizard	turtle
owl	

Warm-Blooded

Mammal	Bird
bear	duck
deer	eagle
fox	owl
rat	shark

Cold-Blooded

Fish	Reptile	Amphibian
trout	lizard	frog
	snake	salamander
	turtle	toad

Find Out

Mammals cool off by sweating. Horses sweat through their skin, and coyotes sweat through their tongues when panting. How do your family pets cool off? How do they stay warm?

Survival

Name _____

An adult frog lays hundreds of eggs at one time. You would think that most ponds would be overrun with frogs. Many of these eggs will hatch, but very few offspring will survive. Most will be eaten by larger animals. Only the fittest survive. The fittest are those that adapt to their environment.

What does adapt mean? adjust to a situation to become more fit for survival

What adaptions help each of these animals survive?

deer quickness, excellent hearing + sense of smell, fawns have camouflage

mouse quickness, small size, can see well in the dark

skunk excellent means of protecting self with scent glands

rabbit speed and good sense of hearing

turtle shell is excellent protection

porcupine sharp quills

Something Special

Create an animal of your own. Give your animal some special defense adaptions.

animal's name _____   enemies _____

habitat _____   defenses _____

food _____

Best Foot Forward

Name _____

Like other animals, birds have adaptions that help them survive. A duck would not swim well if it had the feet of a robin. A woodpecker would not find too many insects if it had the bill of a duck. Can you imagine an owl trying to grab a mouse if it had feet like a duck?

Examine each of the different types of bills and feet pictured below. Match each with one of the advantages listed below. Then use another source to help find a bird that has each feature.

 Bird hawk, eagle
Advantage tearing flesh

 Bird cardinal, sparrow
Advantage cracking seeds

 Bird woodpecker
Advantage probing for insects

 Bird duck
Advantage straining water for food

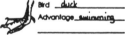 Bird duck
Advantage swimming

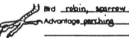 Bird robin, sparrow
Advantage perching

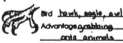 Bird hawk, eagle, owl
Advantage grabbing onto animals

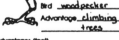 Bird woodpecker
Advantage climbing trees

Advantages (bills)
cracking seeds
straining water for food
tearing flesh
probing for insects

Advantages (feet)
climbing trees
swimming
grabbing onto animals
perching

Something Special

Create your own unique bird. Write a paragraph that describes your bird's habitat, food, enemies, and size. Give your bird a name. Draw a picture of it.

Invertebrates

Name _____

Just three groups of the many kinds of invertebrates are listed below. The first group are arthropods. Arthropods are invertebrates with jointed legs. Insects, spiders, and crustaceans, like lobsters and crabs, belong to this group. Worms are slender, creeping animals with soft bodies and no legs. The last group are mollusks. Mollusks are also soft-bodied, but most have shells for protection. Some mollusks, like the octopus, do not have shells.

Using the words from the word bank, find some examples of invertebrates in the puzzle below. Then list them under the group they belong to.

Word Bank

ant	crayfish	lobster	oyster	squid
clam	earthworm	moth	roundworm	tapeworm
crab	flatworm	octopus	snail	

Arthropods	Worms	Mollusks
ant	earthworm	clam
lobster	roundworm	squid
crab	tapeworm	oyster
moth	flatworm	snail
crayfish		octopus

Fun Fact

The longest known species of giant earthworm is found in South Africa and is 136 cm long!

Answer Key

Animals with a Double Life
Name _____

Amphibians are cold-blooded vertebrates. The word amphibia means to live a double life. Some amphibians live exclusively on land or in the water, while others live in both habitats. Frogs, toads, and salamanders are three of the most common amphibians.

Adult frogs and toads are able to hear you sneak up on them because they have large eardrums, called tympanums. Salamanders do not have eardrums but sense vibrations through their legs.

Frogs and toads develop from eggs that are laid in the water. The larval forms of the frog and toad are called tadpoles. Salamanders hatch from eggs within the adult.

Use the pictures and information above to complete the chart. Make a (✓) in the correct box or boxes.

	Frog	Toad	Salamander
smooth skin	✓		✓
bumpy skin		✓	
nostrils	✓	✓	✓
tympanum	✓	✓	
tail	when tadpoles	when tadpoles	✓
strong hind legs	✓	✓	
backbone	✓	✓	✓
warm-blooded			
cold-blooded	✓	✓	✓

Find Out
Egg-Tadpole-Frog. These are the three stages of a frog's life cycle. What adaptions help the frog get food? What adaptions help the frog breathe in each stage? What adaptions give the frog movement in each stage?

Page 25

Food Chains
Name _____

What did you have for dinner last night? Perhaps it was chicken. A few days ago that chicken was probably eating corn. You eat chicken, the chicken eats the corn, and the corn grows in the sunshine. This is what we call a food chain.

Organisms that make their own food are called producers. Corn is a producer. Green plants are producers because they get their energy from the sun. Organisms that do not make their own food are called consumers.

Name an important food for each animal pictured below. If that food is also an animal, list an important food for that animal. Keep doing this until you run out of animals.

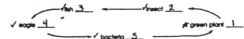

smaller fish	antelope	mouse	steak (cow)	rabbit
insects	grass	corn	grass	plants
plants				

Which organism starts the food chain below? Place a 1 on that line. Number the rest of the food chain in order. Then place a (✓) in front of all the consumers. Place a (*) in front of the producers.

✓ fish 3   ✓ insect 2
✓ eagle 4   * green plant 1
✓ bacteria 5

Something Special
Try to make a food chain with more than four links. What is the longest food chain you can make?

Page 26

More Food Chains
Name _____

In the woodland and aquatic communities, there are a large number of food chains. Study the picture on this page.

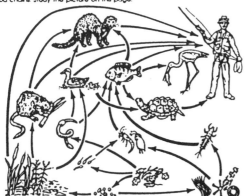

Find at least three food chains in the scene above. List the food chains below.

Food Chain #1	Food Chain #2	Food Chain #3
Answers will vary	otter	man
man	fish	duck
fish	crayfish	plants
worm	tadpole	
leaves	plants	

Find Out
The use of DDT, a chemical insecticide, has been made illegal in many areas. What effect did this poison have on the eagle? How did this affect the eagle population?

Page 27

Meat, Salad, and Casseroles
Name _____

Animals and plants often get their food from different sources. Plants that make their food from sunlight, air, and water are called producers. Animals are consumers; they get their food from other sources. Animals that eat only plants are called herbivores. Carnivores are animals that eat only meat. Omnivores are animals that eat both plants and meat. Which of these are you?

Study the picture below. Then list all the carnivores, herbivores, omnivores, and producers that you can find.

Carnivore	Herbivore	Omnivore	Producer
snake	rabbit	raccoon	cattail
hawk	butterfly	man	grass
turtle	bird	bird	tree

Something Special
Make a food chain using the organisms found in the picture above. Label each member by writing C, H, O, or P over each carnivore, herbivore, omnivore, and producer in the chain.

Page 28

Answer Key

Food Webs

Name _____

Eating would be boring if we ate only one kind of food. Imagine eating oatmeal for breakfast, lunch, and dinner, 365 days a year, for the rest of your life. Most animals, like humans, eat more than one kind of food. This means that most animals are members of more than one food chain. Separate food chains that interlock are called food webs.

Form a food web by drawing arrows from each prey to its predator. Remember—most prey have more than one predator. (Hint: Use a different colored crayon for each food chain.)

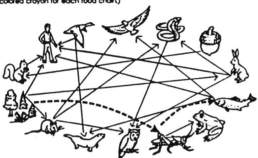

One food chain that you may have found in the food web is this one:
plant ➡️ grasshopper ➡️ trout ➡️ otter

Write two more food chains that you found in your food web. Answers will vary.
1. plant ➡️ mouse ➡️ snake ➡️ owl
   plant ➡️ rabbit ➡️ man
2. plant ➡️ mouse ➡️ eagle

Page 29

Gone for the Winter

Name _____

When the cold winds blow, some animals travel to other regions for the winter. In the spring, they travel back to their summer habitat. This movement is called migration. Some animals migrate to warmer climates to find food. Others, like salmon and whales, migrate to give birth to their young.

Below are three pictures of migration. Choose one of the pictures and write a brief news article for the outdoor section of your newspaper. Good reporters will use the five W's (who, what, where, when, and why) in their articles.

Articles will vary.
_____
_____
_____
_____
_____
_____
_____
_____
_____
_____

Fun Fact

The monarch butterfly flies south for the winter. Many travel from Ontario, Canada to southern Texas—a distance of over 2,400 km.

Page 30

A Winter Snooze

Name _____

When winter arrives, some animals enter a sleep called hibernation. Most hibernators are cold-blooded animals, like snakes, spiders, toads, frogs, and turtles. During hibernation, the animal's heartbeat and breathing slows down to a point where they are hardly noticeable. Body temperature also drops.

Some warm-blooded animals, like bears, raccoons, chipmunks, and groundhogs also hibernate. Bears and raccoons do not sleep soundly. They are easily awakened when hibernating. During hibernation, these animals get energy from fat that they have stored during the late summer.

Finish the crossword puzzle below using the clues and the words in bold for help.

Across
2. Most hibernators are _____ blooded animals.
4. Body _____ drops during hibernation.
6. The _____ beat slows during hibernation.

Down
1. Shelled reptile that hibernates in muddy pond bottoms
2. Small animal that hibernates in underground burrows
3. The time when animals store fat for the winter
5. Bears get their _____ from stored fat.

Crossword answers:
- 2 Across: cold
- 4 Across: temperature
- 6 Across: heart
- 1 Down: turtle
- 2 Down: chipmunk
- 3 Down: summer
- 5 Down: energy

Find Out

Which animals stay in the Arctic during the winter? Which animals migrate from the Arctic?

Page 31

Endangered

Name _____

The only place you will ever see a dodo, a passenger pigeon, or a dinosaur is in a book. These animals no longer live on earth. They are extinct. Today, thousands of animals are in danger of becoming extinct.

The jaguar, polar bear, sperm whale, and African elephant are only a few of the many animals that man is responsible for endangering. These animals are hunted for meat, fur, and trophies.

Some animals are endangered because their habitats are being destroyed by land development. The green sea turtle is endangered because buildings and crowded beaches now take the place of their nesting grounds.

Most recently, man has polluted the environment with pesticides and fertilizers that have poisoned the food of many animals. Insecticides have entered the bald eagle's food chain, causing the eggs to become thin-shelled and break before hatching.

Use another source to find out the names of some other animals that are endangered or extinct. Then fill in the chart below.

Animal	Endangered or Extinct	Why?
_____	_____	Answers will vary. Some possible animals to research are: whooping crane, California Condor, bald eagle, wood bison, key deer, American alligator.
_____	_____	
_____	_____	
_____	_____	
_____	_____	

Something Special

Write an editorial for your local newspaper. State your concern for endangered animals and suggest ways that people could help protect these animals.

Page 32

Answer Key

The Tortoise and the Hare
Name _____

"On your mark. Get set. Go!" The race is on between the tortoise and the hare. Hare speeds away from the starting line at 56 km per hour. Tortoise plods along at less than 1 km per hour.

Many animals depend on their speed to escape from predators. Other animals use their speed to capture their prey. These are the speeds that some animals can travel. Graph the speeds of these animals on the chart below from slowest to fastest. Then answer the questions below.

Animal	Speed (km per hour)
butterfly	19
elephant	40
coyote	72
cheetah	113
grizzly bear	48
housefly	8
salmon	48
sailfish	96
jack rabbit	64
lion	80
human (jogging)	11

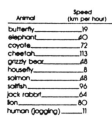
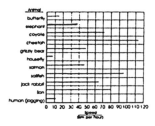

Both the coyote and the rabbit are very fast animals, but each uses its speed in a different way. How does each animal use its speed?

A coyote chases its prey. A rabbit uses its speed to escape its enemies.

The tortoise is not very fast, but it has other adaptions to aid in protection. How does the tortoise protect itself?

It has a hard shell to protect it from its enemies.

Fun Fact
The Olympic athlete can run 43 km per hour, but only for a very short distance and period of time.

Animal Facts
Name _____

Finish the puzzle below using the words from the word bank.

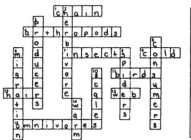

Word Bank
arthropods
birds
chain
cold
consumers
hair
herbivore
insects
migration
omnivores
producers
scales
spiders
warm
web

Across
1. A series of animals that feed on each other is a food ____.
4. Invertebrates with jointed legs
7. Largest group of invertebrates
9. Reptiles are ____-blooded.
11. Feathered, warm-blooded vertebrates
12. Body covering of mammals
13. Interlocking food chains form a food ____.
15. Organisms that eat both plants and animals

Down
2. Animal that eats only plants
3. Organisms that make their own food
5. Organisms that do not make their own food
6. Seasonal movement of animals
8. Arthropods with eight legs, two body sections, and no antennae
10. Body covering of reptiles
14. Birds and mammals are ____-blooded animals.

"Dem Bones, Dem Dry Bones"
Name _____

Use your science book or another source to help.

Matching: Place the letter of the scientific name in the space provided next to the common name.

Label the skeletal system with the scientific name for each bone.

Common Names
- _d_ skull
- _g_ jawbone
- _j_ collarbone
- _c_ shoulder blade
- _k_ tailbone
- _b_ backbones
- _i_ kneecap
- _f_ thigh bone
- _l_ rib
- _a_ hip bone
- _h_ shin bone
- _e_ lower arm bone

Scientific Names
a. pelvis
b. vertebrae
c. scapula
d. cranium
e. radius
f. femur
g. mandible
h. tibia
i. patella
j. clavicle
k. coccyx
l. rib

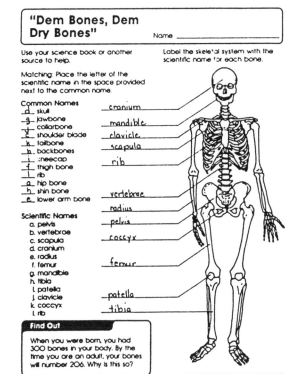

cranium
mandible
clavicle
scapula
rib
vertebrae
radius
pelvis
coccyx
femur
patella
tibia

Find Out
When you were born, you had 300 bones in your body. By the time you are an adult, your bones will number 206. Why is this so?

Muscle Power
Name _____

Use your science book or another source to help.

Fill in the blanks with words from the word bank.

Word Bank
involuntary   smooth   skeletal   tendons
voluntary   cardiac   three

There are _three_ kinds of muscles. Internal organs, such as the intestines, the stomach, and the esophagus are moved by the _smooth_ muscles. The _skeletal_ muscles move your skeleton and external body parts. The heart beat is controlled by the _cardiac_ muscle. Muscles which need a special message from your brain in order to work are called _voluntary_ muscles. Muscles which move automatically, without conscious thought, are called _involuntary_ muscles. The tough cords that connect the skeletal muscles to your bones are called _tendons_.

Fill in the chart.

Activity	Do I need conscious thought to do it?	Voluntary or Involuntary Action	Kind of Muscle
jumping rope	yes	voluntary	skeletal
heart beating	no	involuntary	cardiac
waving	yes	voluntary	skeletal
breathing	no	involuntary	smooth
swallowing food	no	involuntary	smooth
pumping blood	no	involuntary	cardiac
whistling	yes	voluntary	skeletal
running	yes	voluntary	skeletal
digestion	no	involuntary	smooth

Find Out
Who is your Achilles' Tendon named for and why?

Answer Key

Message Transmissions

Name _____

Use your science book or another source to help. Fill in the spaces with words from the word bank.

Your body has its own system for sending messages to your brain. This system of individual nerves and their pathways is found throughout the body. It is called the peripheral nervous system. The peripheral nervous system is a pathway to the brain for your five senses. It also serves your internal organs and helps you respond to your environment.

Messages are sent to the brain through a network of nerve cells called _neurons_. Neurons have long arms, called _axons_ and shorter arms, called _dendrites_.

In order for messages to travel along the pathway, the neurons must connect with each other. This connection is called a _synapse_. Messages enter each neuron through the dendrite. Messages exit the neuron through the axon.

Word Bank

axons
dendrites
synapse
neurons

Color the parts of the nervous system.

brain - gray
spinal cord - blue
nerves - red

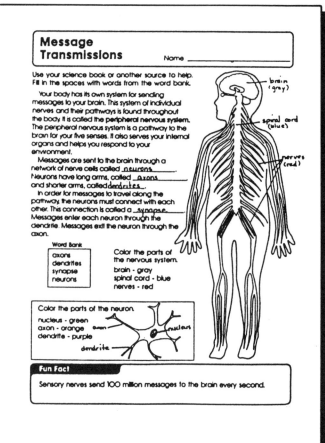

brain (gray)
spinal cord (blue)
nerves (red)

Color the parts of the neuron.

nucleus - green
axon - orange
dendrite - purple

axon
nucleus
dendrite

Fun Fact

Sensory nerves send 100 million messages to the brain every second.

Think Fast

Name _____

While riding your bike down the street, a car suddenly pulls out in front of you. Your eyes send a message to your brain. Your brain sends a message to your muscles to apply the brakes. How long did it take you to stop? This time is called your **reaction time.**

Here is a simple experiment to find out your reaction time. The only materials you will need are a 30 cm ruler and a partner.

1. Place your left arm on your desk with your hand over the edge.
2. Space your thumb and index finger apart a little more than the thickness of the ruler.
3. Your partner will hold one end of the ruler with the other end level with the top of your index finger.
4. Your partner will say "ready," pause a few seconds, and drop the ruler.
5. Catch the ruler and check the distance by reading the level at the bottom of the index finger.
6. Record your results.
7. Now, try the experiment again with your right hand.

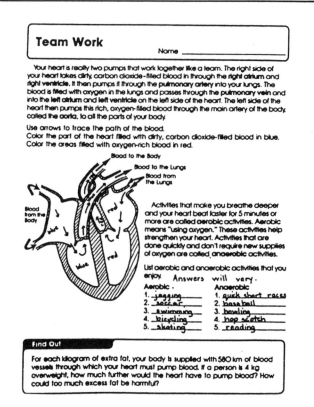

Trial	Left hand	Right hand
1		
2	Answers will vary.	
3		
4		
5		

Average: _____ _____

Which hand had the fastest reaction time? _____

Fun Fact

Nerve impulses, or messages, travel at 100 meters per second!

Interbody Highway System

Name _____

Veins, arteries, and capillaries are the blood vessels that form the fantastic highway system in your body.

Write vein, artery, or capillary in front of the statement that best describes the type of blood vessel.

1. _artery_ carries blood away from the heart
2. _vein_ carries blood back to the heart
3. _capillary_ is the tiniest blood vessel
4. _artery_ carries oxygen-rich blood
5. _capillary_ connects the veins and arteries

Your blood is the vehicle that travels this highway. It transports oxygen, carbon dioxide, food, and waste. Your blood also fights infection and clots to prevent excessive blood loss.

To find out more about blood, do the crossword.

Across

2. Red blood cells are made in _____ marrow.
3. Blood plasma is clear liquid. It is 90 per cent _____.
4. Platelets prevent blood loss by forming a _____
6. Hemoglobin carries _____ to the cells and takes carbon dioxide away from the cells.

Down

1. When you get a cut, white cells fight against _____
4. Hemoglobin gives blood its red _____.
5. Hemoglobin is part of the _____ blood cells.

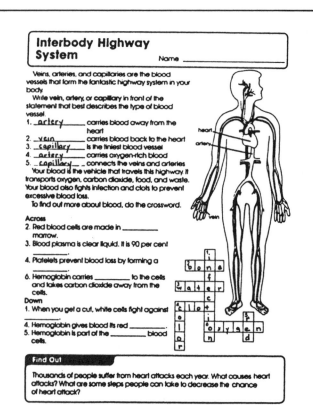

heart
artery
vein

bone
water
clot
color
oxygen

Find Out

Thousands of people suffer from heart attacks each year. What causes heart attacks? What are some steps people can take to decrease the chance of heart attack?

Team Work

Name _____

Your heart is really two pumps that work together like a team. The right side of your heart takes dirty, carbon dioxide-filled blood in through the right atrium and right ventricle. It then pumps it through the pulmonary artery into your lungs. The blood is filled with oxygen in the lungs and passes through the pulmonary vein and into the left atrium and left ventricle on the left side of the heart. The left side of the heart then pumps this rich, oxygen-filled blood through the main artery of the body, called the aorta, to all the parts of your body.

Use arrows to trace the path of the blood.
Color the part of the heart filled with dirty, carbon dioxide-filled blood in blue.
Color the areas filled with oxygen-rich blood in red.

Blood to the Body
Blood to the Lungs
Blood from the Lungs
Blood from the Body

Activities that make you breathe deeper and your heart beat faster for 5 minutes or more are called aerobic activities. Aerobic means "using oxygen." These activities help strengthen your heart. Activities that are done quickly and don't require new supplies of oxygen are called anaerobic activities.

List aerobic and anaerobic activities that you enjoy. Answers will vary.

Aerobic	Anaerobic
1. jogging	1. quick short races
2. soccer	2. baseball
3. swimming	3. bowling
4. bicycling	4. hop scotch
5. skating	5. reading

Find Out

For each kilogram of extra fat, your body is supplied with 580 km of blood vessels through which your heart must pump blood. If a person is 4 kg overweight, how much further would the heart have to pump blood? How could too much excess fat be harmful?

IF8759 Science Enrichment

Pick Up the Beat

Name _____

Your pulse is caused by the stopping and starting of the blood as it rushes through your arteries. You can feel your pulse at any spot an artery is near the surface of the skin. These spots are called pulse points. One pulse point is located on the inside of your wrist.

Name some other pulse points.

near your biceps

side of your neck

ankles

Your pulse rate changes during different kinds of activity. Check your pulse rate after doing these activities.

Activity	Pulse rate for 15 seconds	Multiply by 4	Pulse rate for 1 minute
sitting	Answers will vary.		
hopping 25 times			
hopping 100 times			
lying down			

How does your pulse rate change during exercise?

Your pulse rate increases

Why do you think your pulse rate changes during exercise?

Your muscles need more oxygen. Your heart pumps the blood faster.

Find Out

How does body size affect pulse rate? Check the pulse rates for people of different sizes.

Respiratory System

Name _____

Your breathing, or respiratory, system is made of many parts. Solve the respiratory riddles using the word bank.

1. "I'm the windpipe that brings fresh air to your lungs." trachea
2. "There are 600 million of us tiny air sacs in your lungs." alveoli
3. "Tra-la-la. I'm your voice box." larynx
4. "We branch to the left and right from your windpipe." bronchial tubes
5. "I enter your blood with each breath of fresh air." oxygen
6. "I help squeeze the air out of your lungs." diaphragm

Label the diagram using the words from the word bank.

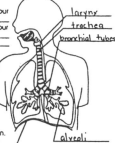

larynx
trachea
bronchial tubes
alveoli
diaphragm

During exercise your body needs more oxygen. Your brain signals your lungs to breathe more quickly and take deeper breaths. Look at the results of the experiment below to answer the questions. Complete the chart.

Activity	Air in each breath (volume)	×	Number of breaths per minute	=	Air in lungs each minute
reading	.5 liters	×	16	=	8 liters
walking	1 liter	×	25	=	25 liters
playing basketball	2 liters	×	60	=	120 liters

Word Bank
alveoli
bronchial tubes
diaphragm
larynx
oxygen
trachea

Which activity makes you breathe fastest? playing basketball
Which activity requires the most oxygen? playing basketball
How much more air per minute does walking take than reading? 17 liters

---

Digestive System

Name _____

Use your science book or another source to help label the parts of the digestive system. Use words from the word bank.

tongue
This tastes food and moves it around in your mouth to be broken down by the teeth and saliva.

esophagus
Food travels down this tube from the mouth to the stomach.

liver
This organ produces the bile which helps break down fats.

gall bladder
Bile produced by the liver is stored here.

duodenum
This is the first section of the small intestine. Food enters here after leaving the stomach. Digestion is still occurring.

appendix
This organ has no function in your body.

salivary glands
Saliva is produced here. Saliva starts changing starches into sugar while still in the mouth.

stomach
Food is stored here for 3-4 hours while digestion is occurring.

pancreas
Produces digestive juices to help break down food in the small intestine.

small intestine
Digestion is completed here. Nutrients are removed from food and enter the blood stream.

large intestine
Solid material which is not used by the body is stored here for at least 24 hours. Water is removed during that time.

rectum
Waste (solid material which has not been digested) is stored here until ready to exit the body.

anus
Waste exits the system through this body opening.

Word Bank

pancreas	large intestine	salivary glands
stomach	esophagus	gall bladder
liver	duodenum	rectum
appendix	small intestine	anus
tongue		

Keep It Covered

Name _____

Your skin does more than cover your body. Your skin does three important jobs. It helps keep your body cool and comfortable. It is a sensor that warns you of danger. And it provides protection from dirt and bacteria.

Label the parts of the cross-section of the skin using words from the word bank. Use your science book or another source to help.

Word Bank
pore
hair
nerve
oil gland
sweat gland
blood vessel
epidermis
dermis

epidermis

dermis

hair
pore
oil gland
blood vessel
nerve
sweat gland

How does your skin help you in the following situations?
heat Sweat glands help keep your body cool.
dirt Skin keeps dirt and bacteria from entering your body.
pain Nerves send pain messages causing you to react and avoid injury.

Fun Fact

Your skin is the thickest where the wear is the heaviest. The skin on the soles of your feet may be almost 5 mm thick and only .05 mm thick over the eye.

Answer Key

The Body's Camera

Name _____

Use your science book or another source to help.
Label the parts of the eye with terms from the word bank.

Word Bank

lens	pupil
cornea	retina
optic nerve	sclera
iris	vitreous humor

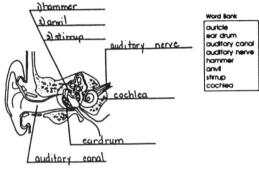

optic nerve
retina
lens
cornea
vitreous humor

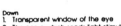

pupil
iris
sclera

Complete the word puzzle using some of the words from the word bank.

Across
3. Dark area which changes size with the amount of light
5. Colored part of the eye
7. White covering of the eye
8. The clear jelly-like humor in the eye

Down
1. Transparent window of the eye
2. The nerve which sends light stimulus to the brain
4. Focuses light onto the retina
6. Sensitive area containing rods and cones

Something Special

Your retina is made up of light-sensitive cells that can be stimulated by pressure. Close your eyes and very gently press on them. The stars that you are seeing are called pressure flashes.

Catching Good Vibes

Name _____

Use your science book or another source to help.
Complete the following sentences using words from the word bank.

The ear honks its horn. The sound waves are collected by your **auricle** and travel down the **auditory canal**. The sound strikes the **ear drum** causing the tight skin to vibrate. Three tiny bones called the **hammer**, **anvil**, and **stirrup** magnify and send the sound to the inner ear. The sound travels to the **cochlea**, a coiled, snail-shaped passage filled with liquid and nerve hairs. The nerve hairs send signals through the **auditory nerve** to the brain.

Label the parts of the ear using words from the word bank.

1) hammer
2) anvil
3) stirrup
auditory nerve
cochlea
eardrum
auditory canal

Word Bank

auricle
ear drum
auditory canal
auditory nerve
hammer
anvil
stirrup
cochlea

Something Special

Answer these riddles.
Which part of your ear has the most rhythm? **eardrum**
What pierces your ears without leaving holes? **sound**

Joe's Tooth: The Inside Story

Name _____

Use your science book or another source to help.

Word Bank

neck
root
crown
cementum
enamel
pulp
dentin

Label the inside parts of Joe's tooth using words from the word bank.

enamel
dentin
pulp
cementum

Label the outside parts of Joe's tooth using words from the word bank.

crown
neck
root

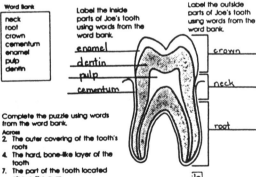

Complete the puzzle using words from the word bank.

Across
2. The outer covering of the tooth's roots
4. The hard, bone-like layer of the tooth
7. The part of the tooth located above the gum

Down
1. Soft tissues, blood vessels, and nerves that fill the inside space of the tooth
3. The tough, outer layer of the tooth
5. The part of the tooth between the crown and the root
6. The part of the tooth embedded in the jaw

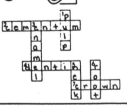

Find Out

We all know that we should brush our teeth after every meal. But did you know that some foods can help keep your teeth clean? What are some of these "natural" toothbrushes?

Nibblers and Chompers

Name _____

Use your science book or another source to help.
Fill in the spaces with words from the word bank.

You have four kinds of **teeth** in your mouth, each with a special job. The large, front teeth are called **incisors**. The incisors are the nippers that help you bite into an apple. The sharp, pointy teeth are **canines**. Canines are used to tear food, like when you chew meat off a bone. The **bicuspids** are large teeth with two points. The **molars** are the large, flat teeth in the back of your mouth. Both the bicuspids and molars are the "millstones" used for grinding food.

Label the teeth on the diagram by printing the following letters on the teeth:
I = Incisors   C = Canines   B = Bicuspids   M = Molars

Word Bank

canines
bicuspids
incisors
molars
teeth

Adult's Upper Teeth   Adult's Lower Teeth

You probably don't have as many teeth as shown in the diagram because you are still growing. As your jaw grows bigger, it makes room for new teeth.

Fill in the following chart.

Type of Teeth	Total Number of Teeth (upper and lower) Adult	You	Type of Chewing
Incisors	8	varies	bite, nip
Canines	4	varies	tear
Bicuspids	8	varies	grind
Molars	12	varies	grind

Total Number of Adult Teeth = **32**

Find Out

What are carnivores, herbivores, and omnivores? What kind of teeth do each of these have? Which one are you?

Answer Key

Cough! Cough!

Name _____

What makes your heart beat faster, replaces the oxygen in your blood with carbon monoxide, makes your blood pressure shoot up, and leaves deadly chemicals in your body—and all in just three seconds? If you answered, "cigarettes," then you are right.

When you inhale smoke, it travels down your windpipe and into your bronchial tubes. These tubes are covered with hair-like parts called cilia. The cilia move back and forth, trying to sweep the smoke dust back up the throat. Cough! Cough! The dust and dirt are out of your body. But cigarette smoke stops these hairs from doing their work. As a result, your lungs become lined with tar. This tar contains chemicals that are harmful to your body.

Cough! Cough! is your body trying to tell you something?

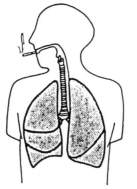

What are three excuses people use for smoking?
1. _Answers will vary. Possible answers:_ My friends smoke.
2. It relaxes me.
3. It helps me lose weight.

What are three reasons why people should not smoke?
1. It could lead to cancer or bad health.
2. It makes breathing more difficult.
3. It leaves a bad odor.

It makes your teeth yellow.

Something Special

Have you ever noticed ads for cigarettes in magazines and on billboards? What is the ad trying to tell you about smoking? Design an advertisement that discourages people from smoking.

Page 49

Your Body and Medicine

Name _____

Drugs can be used as medicine to treat an illness or relieve pain. No one ever knows for sure how your body will respond to any drug. Drugs may cause harmful side effects. If you take an aspirin tablet for a headache, it may relieve your headache, but you might develop an upset stomach or become sleepy.

Drugs that can be bought in a drug store or supermarket are called "over-the-counter" drugs. These drugs may be bought without a doctor's permission. "Prescription" drugs are drugs that are controlled closely by the federal government and may be only bought with a doctor's permission. When using prescription and over-the-counter drugs, you should always read the label carefully.

Study the cough syrup label on this page and answer the questions.
1. Why would someone want to use this medicine? _to stop a cough_
2. How many teaspoons may a 10-year-old take? How often? _1 teaspoon every 4 hours_
3. How many teaspoons may a 10-year-old take in 24 hours? _6 teaspoons_
4. How many teaspoons should an adult take every 4 hours? _2 teaspoons_
5. What should someone do if they still have a bad cough after 1 week? _call a doctor_
6. What warning is given to people who have a high fever? _call a doctor_

WARNING

Medicines can be helpful or harmful. They should never be taken without your parent's knowledge and supervision.

Page 50

Body Trivia

Name _____

Test your knowledge of the human body with these amazing facts.

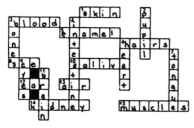

Across
1. 105 sweat glands are found in one square centimeter of your _____
3. Your heart pumps 6,000 liters of this each day.
5. Hardest substance in the human body.
6. The average person has 100,000 of these on his/her head.
8. You do this with your eyes.
10. Your mouth makes ½ liter of this each day.
12. Smallest bones of the body are located here.
13. You breathe 12,000 liters of this each day.
14. Filters 1,500 liters of blood each day.
15. It takes more of these to frown than smile.

Down
2. 17 times more light comes through an expanded one than a narrow one.
3. At birth you have 300, but in adulthood you have 206.
4. "Stomach" rumbles occur here.
6. Strongest muscle in your body.
7. Only part of the body with taste buds.
9. They give you stereo vision.
11. Receives 100 million nerve messages from your senses each second.

Page 51

Solid to the Core?

Name _____

Like a peach, the earth has three layers. You can compare the outer layer, or crust, of the earth to the peach's skin. It is a thin crust of hard rock, from 5 to 70 kilometers thick.

Beneath the crust is the mantle. Like the fleshy part of the peach, it is the thickest layer. The mantle is made of very hot rock that is not liquid, but plastic-like and soft. The mantle is almost 3,000 kilometers thick.

The innermost layer of the earth, the core, is like the peach's pit. The outer core is liquid and most likely made of iron. The outer core is about 2,000 kilometers thick. The inner core is solid and seems to be made of iron and nickel. The inner core is 1,500 kilometers thick.

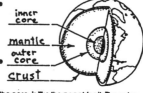

• Use the words in bold above to label the layers of the earth.
• How far is it from the surface to the center of the earth? _6570 km_
• Solve the puzzle below.

Across
1. The earth is nearly 13,000 _____ in diameter.
4. The inner core is made of iron and _____
5. The thinnest layer of the earth.

Down
2. The outer core is made of _____ iron.
3. The thickest layer of the earth, made of hot rock.
5. The innermost layer of the earth.

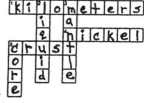

Fun Fact

Nobody has ever drilled or dug through the earth's crust to the mantle. Much of the information we have has been obtained by using a seismograph to measure earthquake waves.

Page 52

Puzzling Theory

Name _____

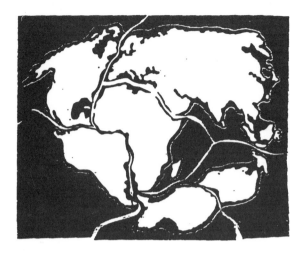

Land Beneath the Ocean

Name _____

The land beneath the ocean has features that are very similar to those that you would see if you traveled across North America.

• Study the picture of the ocean floor. First label the picture and then the descriptions below, using the words from the word bank.

Word Bank
mid-ocean ridge
continental slope
continental shelf
ocean basin
trench

1. **trench** A narrow, deep valley in the ocean basin.
2. **continental slope** A steep incline at the edge of the continental shelf.
3. **mid-ocean ridge** A chain of mountains on the ocean floor.
4. **continental shelf** The part of the ocean floor nearest the continents.
5. **ocean basin** The deepest part of the ocean which contains valleys, plains, and mountains.

Many mountains on the mid-ocean ridges are almost 7,000 meters high, but still don't reach the surface of the ocean.

6. What is formed when an underwater mountain reaches the ocean's surface? **an island**
7. Give an example for number 6. **Ex. The Hawaiian islands are the tops of volcanos. Answers will vary.**
8. Most commercial fishermen do not fish beyond the continental shelf. Why do you think this is so? **The ocean gets so deep that light cannot reach the bottom; fish don't live there because there is no food.**

Find Out
The Mariana Trench in the Pacific Ocean is nearly 11,000 meters deep. Mt. Everest is the highest mountain on earth, but is it higher than the Mariana Trench is deep? How does it compare in size?

"Ping-Ping"

Name _____

The depth of the ocean can be measured using a device called an echo sounder. A sound, "ping," is sent from a ship to the ocean floor. The length of time it takes for the "ping" to strike the ocean floor and bounce back to the ship is recorded. Sound travels in water at a speed of 1,500 meters per second. If a ping takes 6 seconds for a round trip, then a one way trip must take 3 seconds. The depth of the ocean at that point must be 4,500 m (3 sec. x 1,500 m/sec. = 4,500 m).

1. Find the various depths of the ocean using the "ping" soundings on this chart.

2. Using the depths you have listed on the chart, graph your results on the chart below. Connect the points to make a profile of the ocean floor.

3. Put a ✳ on the deep ocean trench.

4. Put an X on the continental slope.

5. Put an M on the undersea mountain.

Sounding	Time (sec.)		Speed (m/sec.)		Depth (m)
1	.4	X	1,500	=	600
2	.4	X	1,500	=	600
3	3	X	1,500	=	4,500
4	2.6	X	1,500	=	3,900
5	3	X	1,500	=	4,500
6	2	X	1,500	=	3,000
7	1	X	1,500	=	1,500
8	2	X	1,500	=	3,000
9	3	X	1,500	=	4,500
10	3.4	X	1,500	=	5,100
11	2	X	1,500	=	3,000
12	7	X	1,500	=	10,500
13	1	X	1,500	=	1,500

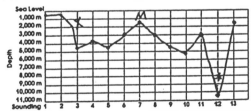

Fun Fact
Only 5% of the world's marine animals live below 1,000 m, in the sea's eternal darkness where sunlight cannot penetrate.

Fire Rocks

Name _____

Deep inside the earth the intense heat causes some rocks to melt. This molten rock, called magma, rises toward the surface of the earth because it is less dense than solid rock. Magma that flows onto the earth's surface is called lava. Some magma cools before it reaches the earth's surface, forming igneous rocks.

Many different types of igneous rocks can be formed, depending on how fast the magma or lava cools. When melted rock cools quickly, very small crystals are formed, causing the new rock to appear glassy. When molten rock cools slowly, large crystals are formed.

• Listed in the word bank are some common igneous rocks. Solve the puzzle, matching each rock with its description. Use what you have read above and information from other sources.

1. Melted rock that comes out of the earth.
2. Melted rock that cooled quickly, forming a black, glassy rock.
3. Greenish-black rock, formed from lava that flowed slowly over the surface.
4. Formed from lava that cooled with hot gases trapped inside, causing it to be filled with air holes.
5. Melted rock below the earth's surface.
6. Magma that cooled slowly, forming large crystals.
7. Lava that cooled slowly, forming large crystals.

Word Bank
pumice   gabbro
granite   magma
lava   obsidian
basalt

1. **lava**
2. **obsidian**
3. **basalt**
4. **pumice**
5. **magma**
6. **granite**
7. **gabbro**

• The hidden word: What do you call a mountain formed by cooled lava? **volcano**

Something Special
It's fun to grow crystals. Rock candy is actually giant sugar crystals. Ask your librarian to help you find a recipe for growing your own super rock candy crystals.

116

Answer Key

Stones of Sand

Name _____

As rivers flow to the sea, they may carry mud, sand, pebbles, and boulders along the way. The river drops this material, called sediment, into the sea. As layers of sediment build up over a period of many years, the great pressure of all these layers changes the sediment into sedimentary rock.

Many different types of sedimentary rock can be formed, depending on the material that is found in the sediment. If the layer of sediment contains large amounts of sand, what kind of rock do you think will be formed? Of course, it will be sandstone.

- Use what you have read above and your science book to help you match the sedimentary rocks with their description.

  a 1. Layers and layers of sand are deposited on the sea bottom to form this rock.

  d 2. A mixture of sand and small pebbles is "cemented" together to form this rock.

  e 3. Living plants in a swamp are covered with sediment and pressed, eventually forming this valuable source of energy.

  c 4. Small sea animals and shells are pressed into this kind of rock.

  b 5. Layers of mud form the most common type of sedimentary rock.

  a. sandstone
  b. shale
  c. limestone
  d. conglomerate
  e. coal

- Sediments settle at different rates of speed. Number these elements in the order that they would settle.

  2 pebbles **1** boulders **3** sand

- What causes sediment to change into hard rock? _The great pressure of layer upon layer of sediment._
- Where would you expect to find sedimentary rocks? _in river beds, lakes, oceans, or where each of these existed at one time._

Fun Fact
As the Mississippi River flows, it carries enough rock each day to fill 40,000 railroad cars.

Changing Rocks

Name _____

With enough pressure and heat, sedimentary and igneous rock can be changed into a new rock. This new kind of rock is called metamorphic, which means "changed in form."

There are a number of ways that metamorphic rock can be formed. One way is when rocks that are buried deep under the earth's surface are flattened by the great pressure from above them. An example of this is when granite is changed into gneiss. Look carefully at the pictures. How has the appearance of the granite changed?

Rock Cycle

The changing of rocks is an ongoing cycle. Look closely at the rock cycle diagram. This cycle shows how rock material is mixed and re-used again and again.

Unscramble the terms to show examples of how igneous and sedimentary rocks can change into metamorphic rock.

1. _SHALE_ changes _SLATE_
   H E S A L into   T A L E S

2. _GRANITE_ changes _GNEISS_
   T R I N E G A into   S I N E G S

3. _LIMESTONE_ changes _MARBLE_
   M O E S T E L N I into   B E L M A R

4. _SANDSTONE_ changes _QUARTZITE_
   T E N O S D A N S into   G U I T A Z E T R

- What three types of rock can an igneous rock change into? _sedimentary, metamorphic, and magma_
- What must happen to an igneous rock before it changes into a sedimentary rock? _It must be worn down into a sediment by wind, rain, or other action._

Find Out
Where is metamorphic rock used in your school? home? community?

Testing Minerals

Name _____

All minerals have certain characteristics, or properties, which distinguish them from other minerals. Minerals can be identified by the testing of these properties. A scratch test is used to determine the property of hardness. Minerals are rated on a scale of one to ten — one is the softest and ten the hardest.

Other properties are also tested. Some of the more common properties that we test are color and luster. Luster is the way a mineral reflects light.

It usually takes many more than the three properties mentioned to identify a mineral, but let's try our skill using only these three properties. (Caution: Some minerals can pass more than one test.)

Hardness Number	Test	Mineral
1	Fingernail scratches it easily	talc
2	Fingernail barely scratches it	gypsum/ kaolinite
3	Copper penny scratches it	calcite/mica
4	Glass scratches it easily	fluorite
5	Steel knife will scratch it easily	apatite/ hornblend
6	It will scratch glass	feldspar
7	It will scratch a steel knife	quartz
8	It will scratch a steel file	topaz
9	It will scratch topaz	corundum
10	It will scratch corundum	diamond

Color	
White:	quartz, feldspar, calcite, mica gypsum, kaolinite, talc
Yellow:	quartz, kaolinite
Black:	hornblend, mica
Gray:	feldspar, gypsum, talc
Colorless:	quartz, calcite, gypsum

Luster	
Glassy:	quartz, feldspar, hornblend, gypsum
Pearly:	calcite, mica, gypsum, talc
Dull:	kaolinite

1. Glassy / Colorless / It will scratch glass. _quartz_

2. Pearly / Colorless / Copper penny scratches it. _calcite_

4. Dull / Yellow / Fingernail barely scratches it. _kaolinite_

7. Glassy / Black / Steel knife will scratch it. _hornblend_

1. Pearly / Black / Copper penny scratches it. _mica_

6. Glassy / Gray / Fingernail barely scratches it. _gypsum_

8. Glassy / Gray / It will scratch glass. _feldspar_

9. Pearly / White / Fingernail scratches it easily. _talc_

It's California's Fault!

Name _____

There are many cracks in the earth's bedrock. These cracks are called faults. One kind of fault is called a strike-slip fault. The rock along one side of the fault moves horizontally in one direction, while the facing rock moves in the opposite direction. Other times, the bedrock on one side of the fault moves upward, while the other side moves down. This is called a dip-slip fault.

The San Andreas Fault is a large strike-slip fault that runs along the coast of California. This famous fault and other smaller faults that form the San Andreas Fault System have been the source of many earthquakes.

strike-slip fault   _dip-slip fault_

1. Label the two types of faults using the words in bold above.
2. On which side of the San Andreas Fault is San Francisco? _east_
3. On which side of the San Andreas Fault is Santa Cruz? _West_
4. The San Andreas Fault's movement has been measured to be as much as 5 cm per year. What might happen to these two cities a million years from now? _They might be neighbors, or suburbs of each other_
5. Many earthquakes occur along the San Andreas Fault. What are some things people can do to protect themselves from earthquakes? _Build better building's, don't build on fault, learn to predict earthquakes_

Fantastic Fact
During the 1906 San Francisco earthquake, roads, fences, and rows of trees that crossed the fault were shifted several meters! One road was shifted almost 7 meters!

©1992 Instructional Fair, Inc.

IF8759 Science Enrichment

Answer Key

Shake, Rattle, and Roll!

Name _____

An earthquake is a movement in the earth's crust. The large blocks of rock along a fault (a crack in the earth) slip past each other. As the blocks of rock slide, their sides may become locked. The strain builds and then becomes too great, causing the rocks to quickly slip past each other. The result is an earthquake. From the origin of the earthquake, called the focus, waves, or vibrations, move out in all directions.

Earthquakes are recorded on a sensitive instrument called a seismograph. The strength of the earthquake is measured on a scale of 1 to 10, with 10 being the strongest. This scale is called the Richter Scale.

Mexico City —	2,600 km
Denver —	1,400 km
Vancouver —	1,600 km

- Seismographs in three cities were able to record the same earthquake. The data showed that the focus of the earthquake was located at different distances from each of the cities. For each city, set your compass for the distance indicated. Draw a circle using the city as its center. Mark the focus by placing an X on the map where the three circles meet.

1. Where do earthquakes usually occur? **along faults**

2. Why might some earthquakes be stronger than others? **more strain is built up between blocks of rocks.**

3. Earthquakes can be felt for great distances, but where is the most damage usually done? **near the focus of the earthquake**

Fantastic Fact
The Richter Scale measures the strength of an earthquake on a scale of 1 to 10. However, an earthquake with a reading of 2 is not twice as strong as a 1, but 32 times as strong. That means that the 1906 San Francisco earthquake, which measured 8.3, was 1 million times stronger than a weak earthquake that measures 4.2 on the Richter Scale.

Page 61

Ring of Fire

Name _____

Deep inside the earth, melted rock called magma moves toward the earth's surface. When the magma reaches the surface, it is called lava.

In a volcano, the magma travels through a tube-like passageway called a conduit, until it reaches an opening in the earth's surface, called a vent. This vent may be in the top of the mountain or it could be a side vent. Sometimes the lava flows out gently, but other times it may explode violently.

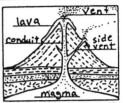

Volcanoes can occur wherever there is a deep crack in the earth's surface. Most volcanoes occur in a large belt that encircles the Pacific Ocean. This belt is called the Ring of Fire.

- Label the parts of the volcano using the words found in bold above.
- Many kinds of material may come out of a volcano. Complete the word puzzle using the clues and the words from the word bank.

Word Bank		
lava	pumice	blocks
gases	tuff	cinder
	ash	

1. Rocks with sharp corners that are blown out from the inside of a volcano.
2. Lava blown into the air, cools into small coarse pieces of rock which are puffed up by gas.
3. Magma that has reached the surface.
4. Lava that is blown apart by gases into light particles that can float in the air.
5. Ash mixed with rain, forming a cement-like rock.
6. Volcanic material that cools into a coarse rock containing many air bubbles, enabling the rock to float in water.
7. Carbon dioxide, sulfur dioxide, and steam are examples of these.

1. b l o c k s
2. c i n d e r
3. l a v a
4. a s h
5. t u f f
6. p u m i c e
7. g a s e s

- Find the hidden name in the word puzzle of the famous active volcano that draws thousands of visitors to the island of Hawaii each year. **Kilauea**

Page 62

Mountain Building

Name _____

fault-block mountains   dome mountains   folded mountains

Mammoth mountains can be found in many places throughout the world. How are these mountains formed?

Most mountains are formed when continental plates collide with each other. The force of the plates pushing against each other causes the crust to bulge up higher and higher, until "waves" of mountains are formed. The mountains that are formed this way are called folded mountains.

Other mountains are formed along faults. Along one side of the fault, the block of crust moves up. Along the other side of the fault, the block of crust moves down. The mountains that are formed from this are called fault-block mountains.

A third type of mountain, formed much in the same way folded mountains are, is a dome mountain. A bulge is formed. However, the bulge is caused by magma from the earth's mantle pushing against the crust.

1. Label the drawings of mountain types using the words in bold.
2. What is the main difference between a folded mountain and a fault-block mountain? **The fault block is forced up by the shifting of blocks of crust along a fault; the folded is forced up by pushing plates.**
3. What are two forces that form mountains? **(1) force of plates moving (2) force of magma pushing up.**

Mountain	Height	Location
McKinley	6,194 m	Alaska
Washington	1,916 m	New Hampshire
Shasta	4,316 m	California
Logan	6,050 m	Canada
Pike's Peak	4,300 m	Colorado

4. The two highest peaks in North America are listed on the chart. Name them and give their heights.
McKinley 6194 m
Logan 6050 m

5. Make a bar graph using the information on the chart. Put the height in meters on the vertical axis, and the name of the mountain on the horizontal axis. **to be done on another piece of paper**

Fun Fact
The Himalaya Mountains of Tibet are the highest mountains on Earth. They were formed 40 million years ago when India drifted away from the east coast of Africa and crashed into Eurasia, piling up the Himalayas which are still growing today.

Page 63

Natural Fountains

Name _____

Geysers, those spectacular natural fountains of spurting hot water, are actually a special kind of hot spring.

Water from rain and snow seeps thousands of meters underground. There the water is heated to 204° or higher, a temperature far above the boiling point of water. This superheated water expands and rises to the surface, where the steam bubbles escape. But from time to time, the bubbles become too abundant to pass up through the water. When this happens, so much steam builds up that the water actually explodes out of a vent in the ground, rising anywhere from 1 m to 60 m into the air.

Yellowstone National Park is known for its geysers and hot springs. Listed below are a few of those geysers.

Geyser	Height	Duration	Interval
Artemisia	9 m	13-15 min.	24-25 hrs.
Beehive	45 m	5-6 min.	8-24 days
Great Fountain	60 m	35-60 min.	8-17 hrs.
Grotto	12 m	1-2 hrs.	4-12 hrs.
Lion	18 m	4 min.	1-2 hrs.
Old Faithful	36 m	2-3 min.	33-93 min.
Riverside	23 m	20 min.	4-8 hrs.
Steady	8 m	steady	steady

1. Graph the height of each geyser.
2. Which geyser erupts the most often? **Steady**
3. Which geyser erupts the least often? **Beehive**
4. Which geyser could possibly have the shortest eruption? **Old Faithful—maybe 2 minutes**
5. Why do you think Old Faithful is the most popular geyser in the park? **Of the large geysers, it erupts most frequently.**

Find Out
Some cities use these natural hot springs in many ways.
(1) How have the people of Reykjavik, Iceland used this geothermal energy?
(2) What are some other ways people can use this source of energy?

Page 64

©1992 Instructional Fair, Inc.   118   IF8759 Science Enrichment

Answer Key

Rivers of Ice

Name _____

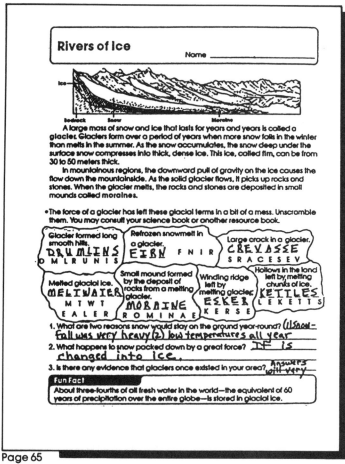

A large mass of snow and ice that lasts for years and years is called a glacier. Glaciers form over a period of years when more snow falls in the winter than melts in the summer. As the snow accumulates, the snow deep under the surface snow compresses into thick, dense ice. This ice, called firn, can be from 30 to 50 meters thick.

In mountainous regions, the downward pull of gravity on the ice causes the flow down the mountainside. As the solid glacier flows, it picks up rocks and stones. When the glacier melts, the rocks and stones are deposited in small mounds called moraines.

• The force of a glacier has left these glacial terms in a bit of a mess. Unscramble them. You may consult your science book or another resource book.

Glacier formed long smooth hills.	Refrozen snowmelt in a glacier.	Large crack in a glacier.
DRUMLINS D M L R U N I S	FIRN F N I R	CREVASSE S R A C E S E V

Melted glacial ice.	Small mound formed by the deposit of rocks from a melting glacier.	Winding ridge left by melting glacier.	Hollows in the land left by melting chunks of ice.
MELTWATER M T W T E A L E R	MORAINE R O M I N A E	ESKER K E R S E	KETTLES L E K E T T S

1. What are two reasons snow would stay on the ground year-round? (1) Snow-fall was very heavy (2) low temperatures all year
2. What happens to snow packed down by a great force? It is changed into ice.
3. Is there any evidence that glaciers once existed in your area? Answers will vary.

Fun Fact
About three-fourths of all fresh water in the world—the equivalent of 60 years of precipitation over the entire globe—is stored in glacial ice.

Page 65

3-D Geologic Map

Name _____

Create your own three-dimensional geologic map.
(1) Make your own key using colors and symbols.
(2) Color each rock formation according to your key.
(3) Cut out the map.
(4) Fold the map to form a box.
(5) Glue the flaps on the inside of the box.

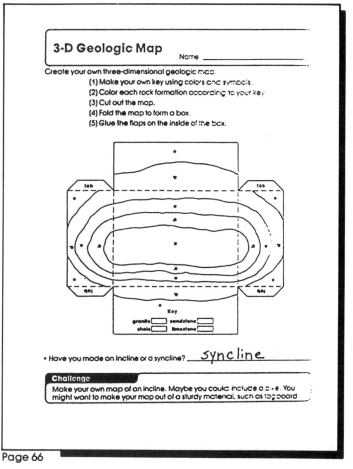

Key

granite		sandstone	
shale		limestone	

• Have you made an incline or a syncline? __syncline__

Challenge
Make your own map of an incline. Maybe you could include a c-e. You might want to make your map out of a sturdy material, such as tagboard.

Page 66

Just Plain Dirt

Name _____

Soil is made of pieces of rocks and minerals that have been broken down by nature over a period of thousands of years.

Soil is found in three layers. The top layer, where plants usually grow, is called topsoil. The second layer, which contains pebbles, sand, and clay, is called subsoil. The bottom layer contains large rocks and is called bedrock.

• How is soil formed? Rocks and minerals are broken down by rain, snow, wind, or other forces of nature.

• The foundation of a very large building often goes all the way down to bedrock. Why? The weight of a large building may cause it to sink & cause it to lean if it is built only on the soil and subsoil.

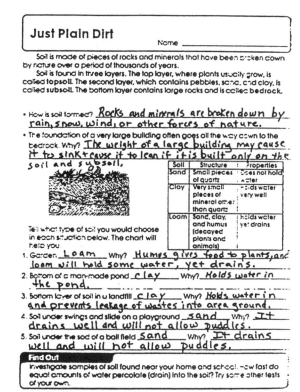

Soil	Structure	Properties
Sand	Small pieces of quartz	Does not hold water
Clay	Very small pieces of mineral other than quartz	Holds water very well
Loam	Sand, clay, and humus (decayed plants and animals)	Holds water yet drains

Tell what type of soil you would choose in each situation below. The chart will help you.

1. Garden __Loam__ Why? Humus gives food to plants, and loam will hold some water, yet drains.
2. Bottom of a man-made pond __clay__ Why? Holds water in the pond.
3. Bottom layer of soil in a landfill __clay__ Why? Holds water in and prevents leakage of wastes into area ground.
4. Soil under swings and slide on a playground __sand__ Why? It drains well and will not allow puddles.
5. Soil under the sod of a ball field __sand__ Why? It drains well and will not allow puddles.

Find Out
Investigate samples of soil found near your home and school. How fast do equal amounts of water percolate (drain) into the soil? Try some other tests of your own.

Page 67

Earth Shattering Review

Name _____

Solve this puzzle using the word bank below.

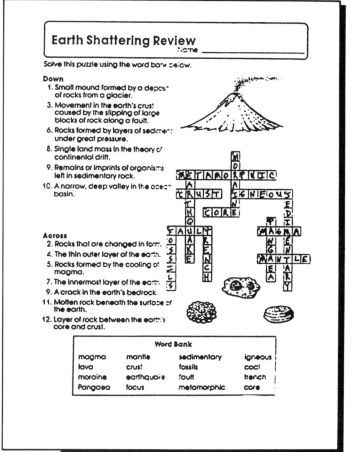

Down
1. Small mound formed by a deposit of rocks from a glacier.
3. Movement in the earth's crust caused by the slipping of large blocks of rock along a fault.
6. Rocks formed by layers of sediment under great pressure.
8. Single land mass in the theory of continental drift.
9. Remains or imprints of organisms left in sedimentary rock.
10. A narrow, deep valley in the ocean basin.

Across
2. Rocks that are changed in form.
4. The thin outer layer of the earth.
5. Rocks formed by the cooling of magma.
7. The innermost layer of the earth.
9. A crack in the earth's bedrock.
11. Molten rock beneath the surface of the earth.
12. Layer of rock between the earth's core and crust.

Word Bank			
magma	mantle	sedimentary	igneous
lava	crust	fossils	coal
moraine	earthquake	fault	trench
Pangaea	focus	metamorphic	core

Page 68

Answer Key

How does the earth move?

Name _____

Hold on tight to your desk. You can't feel it, but you are traveling at a speed of 30 km per hour! The earth is actually traveling at this speed in a circular path around the sun. This path is called its orbit. Each complete orbit, or revolution, around the sun, takes 365¼ days.

The earth has a second type of motion. It spins, or rotates, like a top about an imaginary line that runs from the North Pole to the South Pole. This imaginary line is called the earth's axis. Each complete rotation of the earth takes 24 hours. This motion gives us night and day.

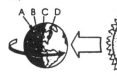

In the picture, City C is experiencing sunrise.

Which city has had sunlight for about one hour? __City D__

Which cities are still dark? __A and B__

Which city will be the next to experience sunrise? __City B__

1. Which movement of the earth gives us our 24-hour day? __rotation__
2. Which movement of the earth gives us our 365¼ day year? __revolution__
3. How many complete rotations has the earth made this month? __will vary__
4. How many complete revolutions has the earth made since you were born? __vary__

Something Special

All of the planets in the Solar System revolve around the sun. Their orbits are not perfect circles. They revolve in an ellipse.

You can draw an ellipse. Place two straight pins about 8 cm apart in a piece of cardboard. Tie the ends of a 25 cm piece of string to the pins. Place your pencil inside the string. Keeping the string tight, draw an ellipse.

Make four different ellipses by changing the length of the string and the distance between the pins. How do the ellipses change?

Page 69

Reasons for the Seasons

Name _____

Do you know why it is hot in the summer and cold in the winter? Because the earth is tilted! The tilt of the earth causes different parts of the earth to get varying amounts of sunlight as it orbits the sun.

Let's take a quick look at the seasons for people living in the Northern Hemisphere. During the summer months, the North Pole is tilted toward the sun. The Northern Hemisphere receives more of the sun's direct rays causing the days to become warmer and the number of daylight hours to increase. Six months later the North Pole is tilted away from the sun. Then the days become colder and the number of daylight hours decreases.

Label the four seasons for the Northern Hemisphere on the diagram below.

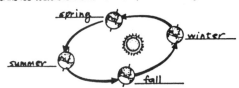

spring

winter

summer

fall

Many things are affected by the changing of the seasons. Complete the chart below using information for your region.

	Outdoor Clothing	Outdoor Activities	Average Daytime Temperature	Time it Gets Dark
Summer	Answers will vary			
Fall				
Winter				
Spring				

Fun Fact

The sun is not exactly at the center of the earth's orbit. During the northern winter, the earth is more than four million kilometers closer to the sun than in the summer. This makes the northern winters warmer than the southern winters.

Page 70

Our Moon

Name _____

On July 20, 1969, Neil Armstrong and Edwin Aldrin left the first footprints on the moon. The astronauts found our moon to be without air, water, plants, or any living things.

The moon is covered with billions of bowl-shaped holes called craters. Some are as small as soup bowls, and others are many kilometers in diameter. Scientists believe the craters were formed when objects traveling in space hit and dented the moon's surface.

When you look at the moon with a telescope, you will see large, flat, smoother areas. Early astronomers believed that these areas were oceans. They called the areas maria, which means "seas" in Latin. Actually, there is no water on the moon. Maria are dry lava beds that were formed by volcanic action on the moon about 3½ million years ago.

Pretend you are an astronaut preparing for a visit to the moon. Decide which items from the list below would be needed or not needed for your visit. Give your reasons.

Item	Needed	Not Needed	Reason
firewood		✓	No air to support burning.
signal whistle		✓	Sound will not travel without air.
matches		✓	No oxygen to support combustion.
water	✓		There is no water on the moon.
raincoat		✓	No rain on the moon.
lightweight equipment		✓	Moon's gravity is 1/6 of earth's.
oxygen	✓		No oxygen on the moon.
food	✓		No food on the moon.

Fun Fact

The moon's gravity is 1/6 of the earth's. A person weighing 54 kilograms on earth would weigh only 9 kilograms on the moon. Find your moon weight by dividing your earth weight by 6.

Earth weight _____ Moon weight _____

Page 71

Changing Faces

Name _____

Everyone has heard about the man in the moon. You have probably even seen pictures of the moon's "face." Have you ever noticed that the moon's face appears to have different shapes at different times of the month? These changes in shape are called the moon's phases. Of course, the moon does not actually change shape, nor does it produce its own light. Do you know what accounts for the moon's shape and light?

As the moon revolves around the earth, we can see different amounts of the moon's lighted part. Study the drawing of the moon's different phases carefully.

③ Half
④ Gibbous
② Crescent
⑤ Full
① New
⑥ Gibbous
⑧ Crescent
⑦ Half

Draw each of the moon's phases as it will be seen from earth. Label each phase.

1 New	2 Waxing Crescent	3 Waxing Half	4 Waxing Gibbous
5 Full	6 Waning Gibbous	7 Waning Half	8 Waning Crescent

Waxing or Waning

As the moon "grows" from the new moon to the full moon, we say the moon is waxing. As it "shrinks" from full moon to new moon, we say it is waning. Label three of your drawings as waning and three as waxing.

Fun Fact

The moon's gravitational pull causes the continent of North America to rise as much as 15 cm when the moon passes over.

Page 72

Answer Key

Space Shadows

Name _____

Crack! It's a high flyball. The sun is shining in the ballplayer's eyes. With one hand raised, the player blocks out the sun, and a shadow appears across his eyes. He can easily see the ball and make the catch.

Just like the ballplayer's outstretched hand, objects in space often cast shadows. Sometimes the moon passes between the earth and the sun. The moon slowly blocks out the sun's light, casting a shadow on the earth. The sky gets dark, the air cools, and for several minutes you can see the stars. This is a solar eclipse.

As the moon travels around the earth, sometimes the earth will cast a shadow on the moon. The full moon darkens as it moves into the earth's shadow. This eclipse, which will last for over an hour, is called a lunar eclipse.

Draw the position of the moon and the shadows for both the solar and lunar eclipses. Label each picture.

Solar eclipse

Lunar eclipse

Complete the following chart by checking the correct box for each statement.	Lunar eclipse	Solar eclipse
earth casts a shadow	✓	
moon casts a shadow		✓
takes place at night	✓	
takes place during the day		✓
moon is blocked out	✓	
sun is blocked out		✓
causes the sky to get dark		✓
causes the air to cool		✓

Something Special

Tribes in the South Pacific had an interesting way of explaining eclipses. They thought that angry gods would swallow the sun or moon and then almost immediately vomit their meal. The sun and moon would continue to shine.

Make up your own legend to explain why eclipses take place.

Exploring Our Solar System

Name _____

You can learn much about the planets in our Solar System by studying the table on this page. Use the information from the table to answer the questions.

Planet	Diameter	Distance from the Sun	Revolution	Rotation
Mercury	4,880 km	57,900,000 km	88 days	59 days
Venus	12,100 km	108,200,000 km	225 days	243 days
Earth	12,756 km	149,600,000 km	365 days	24 hours
Mars	6,794 km	228,000,000 km	687 days	24.5 hours
Jupiter	143,200 km	778,400,000 km	11.9 years	10 hours
Saturn	120,000 km	1,425,600,000 km	29.5 years	11 hours
Uranus	51,800 km	2,867,000,000 km	84 years	16 hours
Neptune	49,500 km	4,486,000,000 km	164 years	18.5 hours
Pluto	2,600 km	5,890,000,000 km	247 years	6.5 days

1. Which planet is closest to the sun? __Mercury__
2. Which planet is farthest from the sun? __Pluto__
3. Which planets are located between Earth and the sun? __Venus, Mercury__
4. Which is the largest planet? __Jupiter__
5. Which is the smallest planet? __Pluto__
6. What is the diameter of Earth? __12,756 km__
7. How long does it take for Pluto to revolve around the sun? __247 years__
8. Which planet takes the least time to revolve around the sun? __Mercury__
9. Which planet revolves around the sun in 365 days? __Earth__
10. Which planet takes the longest to rotate? __Venus__
11. Which planet is almost the same size as Earth? __Venus__
12. Which planet is larger, Pluto or Mars? By how much? __Mars, 4,194 km__

Something Special

Here is an easy way to remember the names of the planets in the order of their distance from the sun. The first letter in each of the words represents one of the planets.

My Very Educated Mother Just Served Us Nine Pizzas

Earth's Nearest Neighbors

Name _____

With a roar of the giant rocket engines, we are pressed tightly to our seats. We are on our way to visit Earth's closest planet neighbors. Our journey takes us first to a planet that looks much like our moon with its craters. It is Mercury, the smallest of our neighboring planets. It is only one-half of Earth's size. There is no air on Mercury to block out the sun's extreme heat. This causes the surface temperature on Mercury to reach 400ºC.

As our spacecraft continues, we sight a planet that is almost the size of Earth. This is Venus, covered with a mist of swirling, yellow clouds. These clouds are made up of droplets of sulfuric acid. We cannot land here because the air is mostly carbon dioxide and the temperature is 470ºC.

Our spacecraft speeds past Earth, quickly approaching a red-colored planet about half the size of Earth. Its surface is dry and desert-like and covered with craters. This is Mars, with its violent dust storms. Be sure to keep an eye out for Martians! The temperature on the surface is 26ºC. But we won't see any life here because the air is 100 times thinner than Earth's and is 95 per cent carbon dioxide.

Complete the chart below using the information you gathered on your visit to the neighboring planets.

	Daytime Temperature	Size Compared to Earth	Atmosphere	Surface
Mercury	400°C	½ the size	no air	craters
Venus	470°C	almost same size	mostly carbon dioxide	can't see, clouds
Earth	varies	same	air	mountains, plains, water
Mars	26°C	½ the size	mostly carbon dioxide	dry, desert-like

Fun Fact

Because Venus travels in an orbit inside the earth's orbit, it appears to us in phases. Its night side faces Earth every 584 days.

The Outer Planets

Name _____

Our spacecraft pushes on to explore the two largest planets in our Solar System.

We are approaching the largest planet, Jupiter. It is eleven times wider than Earth. If it were hollow, it could hold 1,300 Earths inside! We can see Jupiter's rapidly changing bands of clouds and brilliant flashes of lightning.

It is extremely warm; Jupiter gives off twice as much heat as it receives from the sun. The Great Red Spot on the surface is a tremendous storm, 14,000 km wide and 40,000 km long. It travels completely around the planet every six days. Beneath the thick clouds, Jupiter is a great, spinning ball of liquid ammonia and methane gases.

We are now approaching one of the most fantastic sights of our journey–the giant rings of Saturn. The rings sparkle in the sunlight as they circle the glowing, yellow planet. As we get closer to the rings, we notice that they are actually particles of ice and ice-covered rock orbiting the planet. The rings are over 65,000 km wide but only a few kilometers thick. Like Jupiter, Saturn seems to be covered with a thick covering of clouds. High winds are blowing, and the temperature in the clouds is -190ºC.

1. Which is the largest planet in the Solar System? __Jupiter__
2. Which is the second largest? __Saturn__
3. What are Saturn's great rings? __particles of ice and ice-covered rocks__
4. What is Jupiter's "Great Red Spot"? __a tremendous storm__
5. How are Saturn and Jupiter alike? __Both are covered with clouds.__
6. Could you live on Jupiter? Why or why not? __You could not live on Jupiter because it is covered with ammonia and methane gas.__

Fun Fact

Even though Saturn is the second largest planet, it has the lowest density of all the planets. If you could put Saturn in a giant tub of water, it would float!

---

121   IF8759 Science Enrichment

The Edge of the Solar System

Name _____

Three distant planets remain for us to visit before we head back to Earth. Very little is known about these planets because of their distance from the sun.

Our spaceship is approaching the greenish-blue planet of Uranus. It appears to be about four times the diameter of Earth. It has nine rings, much like Saturn's. The planet is covered with clouds that are made up of hydrogen, helium, and methane gas. As we leave Uranus, we can count five moons orbiting the planet.

We are now 4.5 billion kilometers from Earth and are approaching the eighth planet, Neptune. Neptune is similar in size to Uranus. It is also covered with a thick, cloud atmosphere of hydrogen and methane gas.

As we get nearer to Pluto, we are now at the edge of the Solar System. If we look back, our sun appears like a bright star in the sky. Pluto is so far away from the sun that the temperature is almost absolute zero, the point at which there is no heat at all.

Use the clues to fill in the puzzle and find the secret word.

1. Uranus has five _____
2. Planet farthest from the sun
3. Planet with nine rings
4. Neptune is covered with _____
5. Eighth planet from the sun

The secret word is _space_

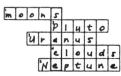

m o o n s
p l u t o
Ur a n u s
c l o u d s
Neptune

Find Out

Uranus lies on its side as it revolves around the sun once every 84 years. For 42 years, one pole is in the sunlight, and the other is in darkness. During the next 42 years, the conditions reverse. Where do the longest nights and days occur on Earth? When does it happen? Why does it happen?

Comets, Asteroids, and Meteors

Name _____

There are other objects in our Solar System besides planets, moons, and the sun. You might have seen some of them streaking by if you have ever stared at the evening sky.

Comets are like "dirty snowballs." A comet is made up of frozen gas (the snow) and dust particles (the dirt). It shines by reflecting the sun's light as it travels in a stretched-out orbit around the sun. As a comet gets closer to the sun, it melts and forms a "tail."

Between the orbits of Jupiter and Mars are thousands of rocky objects, called asteroids, orbiting the sun. Asteroids, some as large as 1,000 km long, are believed to be pieces of a planet that broke apart.

Meteors are streaks of light made by chunks of stone or metal traveling through Earth's atmosphere and burning up. If a meteor strikes the earth, it is called a meteorite. Some people call meteors "shooting stars."

Label the different parts of the Solar System: the sun, the planets, the comet, and the asteroids.

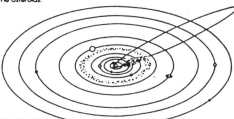

Complete the chart by placing a (✓) in the appropriate box.

	Meteor	Asteroid	Comet
frozen ball of dust			✓
orbits the sun		✓	✓
shooting star	✓		
burns up in Earth's atmosphere	✓		
orbits between Mars and Jupiter		✓	
appears as a streak in the sky	✓		✓
is visible in our sky	✓	✓	✓

Magnitude

Name _____

The stars that you see on a clear night seem to be closer than they really are. Light from the sun, the closest star to Earth, takes 8.3 minutes to reach us. Light from the next closest star, Proxima Centauri, takes 4.3 years to reach us. Proxima Centauri is not even visible without the aid of a telescope.

All of the stars in the sky do not look alike. The most visible difference is in the brightness of the stars. The measure of brightness is called magnitude. The magnitude of a star is determined by its size, distance from Earth, and its temperature.

Stars are balls of hot gases. The color of a star helps us determine its temperature. Red stars are the coldest stars, with a surface temperature of 3,000°C. The hottest stars that can be seen are blue stars. Their temperature is over 20,000°C. White stars are over 10,000°C. Our sun is a yellow star with a surface temperature of 5,500°C.

Use what you have learned about temperature and star color to color the stars.

Red 3,000°C   Yellow 5,000°C   white 10,000°C   blue 20,000°C

What three factors determine a star's magnitude?

size   _distance from Earth_   _temperature_

Two stars are the same color and distance from Earth, but their size is different. Which star will have the greater magnitude? _The larger of the two_

Use the information from the chart to make a graph showing the temperature of the four stars.

Star	Color	Temperature
Rigel	Blue-white	12,000°C
Sun	Yellow	5,500°C
Betelgeuse	Red	3,000°C
Sirius	White	10,500°C

A Star is Born

Name _____

Nobody has ever lived long enough to see a star being "born" and then "die." The changes in a star's life take place over billions of years. Let's look at the stages of a typical star.

A star is formed from a swirling nebula, or cloud of dust and gas, in space. The forces of gravity press the matter in the nebula together. When the matter is pressed tightly enough, it gets hotter and hotter, until a new star is born. This new star is large and cool—although cool is 3,000°C. The new star has a red glow.

If the star continues to compress, the matter may become one of several different colors. It may become blue, white, yellow, or red. In terms of star heat, this is hot, warm, lukewarm, or cool. Our sun is a yellow star. It is hotter than a red star, but cooler than a white star.

1. How long is the life span of a star? _Billions of years_
2. What is a nebula? _Swirling cloud of dust and gas in space._
3. What color is the sun? _yellow_
4. Which color stars are hotter than our sun? Cooler than our sun? _Hotter stars are blue and white. Cooler stars are red._

Number the stages of the birth of a star in the correct order.

_4_ The matter in the young star continues to compress and get hotter.
_1_ The nebula is a swirling mass of dust and gas.
_3_ The newly born star is a cool 3,000°C.
_2_ Gravity forces dust and gases of the nebula to press together.
_5_ The star becomes a new color as it gets hotter.

Find Out

Our sun is a five billion year-old star that has been using up 4½ billion tons of hydrogen every second. How much hydrogen does the sun use in one day?

Answer Key

Star Death

Name _____

As stars get older, they go through changes. A star begins "old age" when its central core of hydrogen has become all helium. Its energy source is gone. Gravity squeezes the center core tight, while the outer layers begin to expand and cool to a dull red. The star becomes a red giant.

The outer layer forms a ring nebula that disappears into space leaving behind a super-collapsed core, about the size of a planet. The core becomes hotter as it collapses and forms a small, white star called a white dwarf. The white dwarf is so dense that a teaspoon of material would weigh almost one ton.

Because the white dwarf has no energy left, it grows dimmer and dimmer until it is a cold, black sphere called a black dwarf.

As you grow older, you can see changes over periods of months and years. You can't see the changes in stars. Stars change over periods of millions, and sometimes billions, of years.

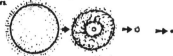

1. Why do stars die? _They die because their energy is gone._

2. Could you see a black dwarf? Why or why not? _No, because it no longer gives off light._

Number the stages of a dying star in the correct order.
  4 The white dwarf becomes cooler and dimmer.
  2 The outer layer of the star expands while the core squeezes tight, forming a red giant.
  5 The star becomes a cold, black sphere in space.
  1 The star uses its last remaining supply of hydrogen.
  3 The outer layer of the red giant forms a ring nebula.

Fun Fact
Sometimes massive stars explode leaving behind a super-dense core called a neutron star. The gravity is so strong on a neutron star, that the average person would weigh about 13½ billion tons if standing on the neutron star's surface!

Black Holes

Name _____

Imagine a star with gravity so strong that nothing can escape from it, not even light. These stars are called black holes.

When a massive star begins to burn out, it collapses. A star ten times the size of our sun will shrink to a sphere about 60 km in diameter. It becomes so dense and the gravitational pull so strong, that the star disappears! Anything that passes close to it in space will be sucked in and never get out!

How do astronomers look for black holes if they can't be seen? They look indirectly. A black hole pulls in matter from nearby stars. As the matter disappears, it sends out strong bursts of x-rays. Astronomers look for these x-ray signals. The most promising candidate for a black hole is the x-ray source known as Cygnus X-1.

Secret Message
The black hole below has swallowed some of the planets of the Solar System. Shade in the names of the planets. The letters that are not shaded will help you solve the secret message.

_IF BLACK
HOLES
EXIST,
NOBODY
CAN SEE
THEM._

Something Special
Black holes seem almost like science fiction. Write a science fiction newspaper article using the headline.

STAR TIMES
Explorer XII Last Seen Near Cygnus X-1

Pictures in the Stars

Name _____

Have you ever made pictures by drawing dot-to-dot? On a clear night, lie on your back and gaze up at the hundreds of twinkling stars. Try to imagine different pictures by drawing lines from star to star. Hundreds of years ago, people drew pictures with the stars in this same way. These pictures are called constellations.

Many of the constellations get their names from Greek mythology. One well-known constellation of the winter skies is Orion, the mighty hunter of Greek mythology.

We can use constellations to help locate special stars. The Big Dipper is a constellation that can help you locate Polaris, the North Star. With your eye, make an imaginary line from the two stars on the end of the Dipper's cup. This line will point to the Dipper's cup.

1. What is a constellation? _An imaginary picture made with stars._

2. How can a constellation be helpful to the stargazer? _They can help you locate specific stars_

Many constellations are hard to picture. Below are the four star patterns that are also shown above. Identify the constellations by their common name. Then connect the stars to form a new constellation of your own. Give this new constellation a name.

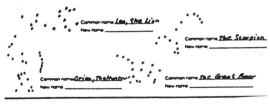

Common name _Leo, the Lion_
New name _____

Common name _The Scorpion_
New name _____

Common name _Orion, The Hunter_
New name _____

Common name _The Great Bear_
New name _____

The Zodiac

Name _____

Ancient astronomers noticed that certain constellations always came up in the east just before sunrise. This was because they were found in the same path that was traced by the sun across the sky. The path made by these constellations actually formed a belt that circled around the heavens. This belt was divided into twelve equal parts, each containing one major constellation.

Most of the constellations that appeared in this belt were named after animals. The early Greeks called this belt Zodiakos Kyklos, or "circle of animals." We call it the Zodiac for short.

The Zodiac was eventually used by fortune-tellers, known as astrologers, to tell the fortune of a person born under a particular Zodiac sign. (Each Zodiac sign is associated with a specific time period in the year.) The reading by an astrologer is called a horoscope.

Circle the Latin names of the twelve constellations of the Zodiac in the wordsearch.

Word Bank
Aquarius	Libra
Aries	Pisces
Cancer	Sagittarius
Capricorn	Scorpio
Gemini	Taurus
Leo	Virgo

Match each Latin name with its English translation.

Aries	The Ram	_Libra_	The Scales
Taurus	The Bull	_Scorpio_	The Scorpion
Gemini	The Twins	_Sagittarius_	The Archer
Cancer	The Crab	_Capricorn_	The Goat
Leo	The Lion	_Aquarius_	The Water Carrier
Virgo	The Virgin	_Pisces_	The Fish

Find Out
Astrology is a "pseudo-science." What is a pseudo-science? Can you name other pseudo-sciences?

IF8759 Science Enrichment

Answer Key

Space Puzzle

Name _____

Use the clues and words from the word blank to complete the puzzle. Use the numbered letters to solve the riddle at the bottom of the page.

Word Bank:
astronomer	fall	Mercury	Pluto	sun
axis	fusion	meteorite	red	
Centauri	hydrogen	moon	rotation	
Earth	maria	orbit	shuttle	

1. A star's energy comes from nuclear **fusion**
2. The only planet with life is **Earth**.
3. The path of a planet around the sun is its **orbit**.
4. Earth's largest satellite is the **moon**.
5. The autumnal equinox is the first day of **fall**.
6. The planet farthest away from the sun is **Pluto**.
7. The closest planet to the sun is **Mercury**.
8. A meteor that lands on the earth is a **meteorite**.
9. A scientist who studies the Universe is an **astronomer**.
10. A star's fuel is **hydrogen**.
11. The star closest to the earth is the **sun**.
12. Oceans on the moon are called **maria**.
13. A space **shuttle** is a reusable space craft.
14. The closest star to our solar system is Proxima **Centauri**.
15. The color of a dying star is **red**.
16. The spinning movement of a planet is its **rotation**.
17. The imaginary line from the North Pole to the South Pole is the Earth's **axis**.

Something Special

How do creatures from outer space drink their tea?
from flying saucers!

What Is Weather?

Name _____

"Today it will be sunny and warm with increasing cloudiness in the late afternoon." The changing condition in the atmosphere (the layer of air that surrounds the earth) is called weather.

Weather is caused by the uneven heating of the atmosphere. For example, where the sun's rays strike the earth at a slant, the earth is heated less than where the sun's rays strike directly. Also, water and land absorb heat and cool off at different rates.

Energy from the sun, called solar energy, causes weather. Look at the picture. What happens to the sun's energy?

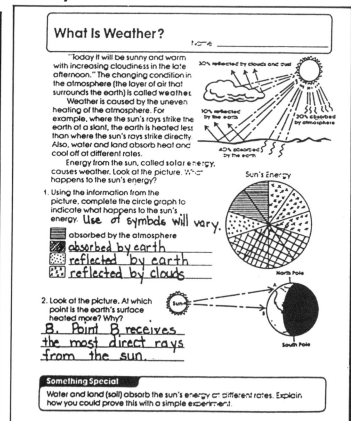

1. Using the information from the picture, complete the circle graph to indicate what happens to the sun's energy. **Use of symbols will vary.**

   ▓ absorbed by the atmosphere
   ▨ **absorbed by earth**
   ▫ **reflected by earth**
   ▦ **reflected by clouds**

2. Look at the picture. At which point is the earth's surface heated more? Why?
   B. Point B receives the most direct rays from the sun.

Something Special

Water and land (soil) absorb the sun's energy at different rates. Explain how you could prove this with a simple experiment.

Pop!

Name _____

Have you ever felt your ears "pop" while riding down a large hill in a car? Your ears have sensed a change in air pressure.

Air pressure is the force of all the air in the atmosphere pushing down on the surface of the earth. When air is heated, the particles of air move farther apart, and the air becomes less dense. This lowers the air pressure because there are fewer air particles over a certain part of the earth. This is called a low pressure area. Water vapor also lowers air pressure because water vapor is a gas and is not as dense as air.

Cool air is more dense than warm air. It forms a high pressure area.

Complete the puzzle.
1. Air pressure is the _____ of air on the earth's surface.
2. Water _____ lowers air pressure.
3. Warm air _____ air pressure.
4. Air in the earth's _____ pushes down on the earth's surface.
5. Cool air forms _____ pressure areas.

Crossword answers: VAPOR, FORCE, ATMOSPHERE, LOWERS, HIGH

High pressure and low pressure areas are usually located on a weather map with the symbols H and L. Cut out the weather map in the newspaper. Copy it on this map.

Fun Fact

High pressure areas on a weather map usually mean fair weather. Low pressure areas often bring changing weather.

Where the Action Is

Name _____

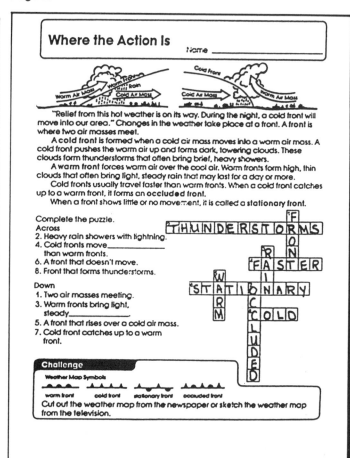

"Relief from this hot weather is on its way. During the night, a cold front will move into our area." Changes in the weather take place at a front. A front is where two air masses meet.

A cold front is formed when a cold air mass moves into a warm air mass. A cold front pushes the warm air up and forms dark, towering clouds. These clouds form thunderstorms that often bring brief, heavy showers.

A warm front forces warm air over the cool air. Warm fronts form high, thin clouds that often bring light, steady rain that may last for a day or more.

Cold fronts usually travel faster than warm fronts. When a cold front catches up to a warm front, it forms an occluded front.

When a front shows little or no movement, it is called a stationary front.

Complete the puzzle.
Across
2. Heavy rain showers with lightning.
4. Cold fronts move_____ than warm fronts.
6. A front that doesn't move.
8. Front that forms thunderstorms.

Down
1. Two air masses meeting.
3. Warm fronts bring light, steady_____
5. A front that rises over a cold air mass.
7. Cold front catches up to a warm front.

Crossword answers: THUNDERSTORMS, FASTER, STATIONARY, FRONT, WARM, COLD, OCCLUDED

Challenge

Weather Map Symbols
warm front   cold front   stationary front   occluded front

Cut out the weather map from the newspaper or sketch the weather map from the television.

Answer Key

Blowing in the Wind

Name _____

Do the winds in your area seem to blow from the same direction everyday? The most common wind in your area is called the prevailing wind.

Weather records sometimes show the prevailing winds with a wind rose. A wind rose is made of a dot with a set of lines, looking like the spokes on a wheel. The length of each line shows the speed of the wind. The position of the line indicates the direction from which the wind blows.

Look carefully at the wind rose at the right. From what direction does the strongest wind usually blow? If you said the northwest, you are correct. Wind roses can be very helpful when trying to predict the direction that pollution such as smog, smoke, and noise will move in your area.

Look at the map below. Pretend that you are a city developer. Considering smog, noise, and smells, where would you locate the listed structures in your town? Draw the symbols for each structure on the map and give your reason.

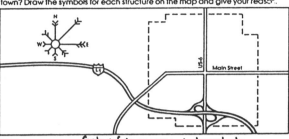

- ▭ shopping center — Center of town, easy to travel to
- ⌂⌂ housing development — In NE to receive clean air
- ✈ airport — (NE,NW,SE) away from smoke, not where noise will bother houses
- 🗑 landfill (dump) — Far SW. smells will not blow on houses or factories
- 🏭 smoky, noisy factory — SW. smoke will not blow on houses
- 🏭 clean, noisy factory — SW. noise will be away from houses
- 🏭 clean, quiet factory — NW, SE. may be a little closer to houses
- ⛲ park — Locate in area not affected by smoke or smell

Gentle Breeze

Name _____

"Today the wind will be a gentle breeze from the northwest." The direction of a wind is always named for the direction from which the wind blows. Meteorologists use a weather vane to find the wind direction. The arrow points into the wind. What direction is the wind in the picture coming from?

__North__

Wind speed can be described in many ways. It can be described with words like "gentle breezes," "strong wind," or "calm." Other times it can be given in kilometers or miles per hour as measured with an anemometer. The Beaufort Scale shown on this page is often used to describe wind speed.

1. Keep a record of the wind for this week. Write the Beaufort number and symbol.

MON.	TUE.	WED.	THUR.	FRI.

2. On a weather map, the wind symbol gives both the direction and speed. Write the direction and type of wind for these cities.

City	Wind Direction	Type of Wind
Miami	East	whole gale
Chicago	West	gentle breeze
Denver	Northwest	mod. breeze
L.A.	South	light air
Seattle	West	light breeze
Toronto	North	mod. breeze

Beaufort Wind Scale

Number and Symbol	Description	Type of Wind	Wind Speed km/h
⊙	smoke rises straight up	calm	0-1
—	smoke drifts	light air	1-5
	wind felt on face, leaves rustle	light breeze	6-12
	flag blows straight out	gentle breeze	13-18
	loose papers blow	moderate breeze	19-28
	small trees sway	fresh breeze	29-38
	hats blow off, branches move	strong breeze	39-50
	difficult to walk against wind	moderate gale	51-61
	small branches break off trees	fresh gale	62-74
	damage to buildings	strong gale	75-87
	trees uprooted	whole gale	88-101

Hot and Sticky

Name _____

"Our hot, sticky weather will continue today with a relative humidity of 83%." Relative humidity is the amount of water vapor that the air can hold at a certain temperature. A relative humidity of 90% is very humid and uncomfortable.

Relative humidity is measured with a hygrometer, which is made of wet bulb and dry bulb thermometers. If the humidity is low, the water on the wet bulb thermometer will evaporate and cool the thermometer. By finding the difference between the temperatures on both thermometers and using a chart, you can find the relative humidity.

1. Michelle recorded the following data over a period of one week. Use the table to find the relative humidity.

Day	Dry Temp.	Wet Temp.	Difference	Relative Humidity
Mon.	21°	20°	1°	91%
Tue.	23°	21°	2°	84%
Wed.	22°	20°	2°	83%
Thur.	21°	17°	4°	67%
Fri.	21°	16°	5°	60%
Sat.	20°	16°	4°	66%
Sun.	20°	17°	3°	74%

Dry bulb temp. °C	Difference between wet and dry temperatures							
	1°	2°	3°	4°	5°	6°	7°	8°
15°	90	80	71	61	53	44	36	27
16°	90	81	71	63	54	46	38	30
17°	90	81	72	64	55	47	40	32
18°	91	82	73	65	57	49	41	34
19°	91	82	74	65	58	50	43	36
20°	91	83	74	66	59	51	44	37
21°	91	83	75	67	60	53	46	39
22°	92	83	76	68	61	54	47	40
23°	92	84	76	69	62	55	48	42
24°	92	84	77	69	62	56	49	43
25°	92	84	77	70	63	57	50	44
26°	92	85	78	71	64	58	51	46
27°	92	85	78	71	65	58	52	47

2. Use Michelle's data to make a graph of the relative humidity.

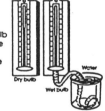

Rain, Snow, Sleet and Hail

Name _____

Neither rain, snow, sleet, nor hail will stop the dedicated postmen and postwomen. They will not be stopped by any form of precipitation. Precipitation is water vapor that condenses and falls to the earth.

All precipitation starts as water vapor. The water vapor cools and then condenses, forming water droplets or ice crystals depending on the temperature. The form of the precipitation depends on the temperature, air currents, and the humidity.

Identify each form of precipitation with the correct symbol.

≡	,	●	▽	✳	⊙	▽
fog	drizzle	rain	heavy rain	snow	sleet	hail

1. ,	light mist of droplets falling to the earth	4. ✳	vapor that changes directly into a solid because of freezing temperatures	7. △▽	droplets that freeze and are bounced up and down through the cloud, building layers
2. △	droplets that freeze as they get closer to the ground	5. ●	water vapor that forms droplets and falls to the earth	
3. ▽	large amount of droplets falling to the earth	6. ≡	clouds that form close to the ground	

Record the precipitation twice each day this week using the correct symbols.

Sunday		Monday		Tuesday		Wednesday		Thursday		Friday		Saturday	
AM	PM	AM	PM	AM	PM	AM	PM	AM	PM	AM	PM	AM	PM

Fun Fact

The wettest place in the world is on the island of Maui in Hawaii. It rains 350 days of the year!

Answer Key

Partly Cloudy

Name _____

"This morning the skies will be clear with clouds forming in the early afternoon." Clouds are formed when a rising mass of air is cooled. Rising warm air reaches levels where the air pressure is lower, causing the air to expand. As air expands, it uses up heat energy, and the air becomes colder. If the air is cooled below the dew point, the water vapor in the air condenses as tiny droplets or ice crystals and forms a cloud.

Crossword puzzle:
C O O L E D
O   D E W
N
D
H E A T
N
S
E X P A N D
S

1. Water vapor _____ to form water droplets
2. Warm, moist air condenses when it is _____
3. Water vapor forms droplets when it is cooled below the _____ point.
4. Expanding air uses up _____ energy.
5. Lower air pressure causes the warm air to _____

Meteorologists use shaded circle symbols to record the amount of cloud cover in the sky. The location of the clouds in the sky can also be shown by shading the matching part of the circle.

N
W   E
S
1/4 cover in the southeast

● completely overcast
◔ 3/4 covered
◑ 1/2 covered
◕ 1/4 covered
⊘ scattered clouds
○ no clouds

Record the cloud cover for one week using the symbols above.

Sunday	Monday	Tuesday	Wednesday	Thursday	Friday	Saturday
○	○	○	○	○	○	○

Page 93

Cloudy Weather

Name _____

There are three basic types of clouds.
Cirrus — High, thin, feathery clouds. They often mean good weather.
Stratus — Low clouds that form layers. They usually mean stormy weather.
Cumulus — Puffy clouds that form in heaps. They usually mean fair weather.
Two other words help describe the three basic types of clouds.
Nimbus or nimbo means rain.
Alto means forming in the middle layer in the sky.

Most clouds are a combination of the three basic types of clouds. The cloud types and their symbols are listed below.

High Clouds	Middle Clouds	Low Clouds	Clouds found at all heights
Cirrus	Altocumulus	Stratocumulus	Cumulus
Cirrocumulus	Altostratus	Stratus	Cumulonimbus
Cirrostratus		Nimbostratus	

• Use the chart, symbols, and descriptions of the three basic types of clouds to identify the clouds described below.

1. high, thin, bumpy clouds   Cirrocumulus
2. low, gray rain clouds   Nimbostratus
3. puffy rain clouds   Cumulonimbus
4. high, thin, layered clouds   Cirrostratus

• Record the types of clouds and describe the weather for one week.

	Sun.	Mon.	Tues.	Wed.	Thur.	Fri.	Sat.
Cloud							
Weather							

Page 94

Br-r-r-r-r

Name _____

On a hot summer day, one of the most comfortable places to be is sitting in front of a fan. Why does this make you feel cooler? The air the fan is blowing is the same temperature as the air in the rest of the room. But the wind from the fan evaporates your perspiration, which lowers the temperature of your skin.

Outside, the wind can have the same cooling effect. This is called wind chill. Wind chill is found on a wind chill chart using the temperature and the wind speed.

1. Ryan collected the following data. Find the wind chill.

Day	Wind Speed	Temp.	Wind Chill
Sun.	8 km/hr	10°	8°
Mon.	32 km/hr	- 1°	-15°
Tues.	24 km/hr	4°	-5°
Wed.	calm	- 1°	-1°
Thur.	8 km/hr	-17°	-20°
Fri.	16 km/hr	- 6°	-15°
Sat.	40 km/hr	- 12°	-34°

Wind Chill Chart
Thermometer Reading °C

Wind Speed (km/hr)	10°	4°	-1°	-6°	-12°	-17°	-23°
calm	10°	4°	-1°	-6°	-12°	-17°	-23°
8	8°	2°	-2°	-8°	-14°	-20°	-26°
16	4°	-2°	-8°	-15°	-22°	-29°	-36°
24	2°	-5°	-12°	-20°	-27°	-38°	-43°
32	0°	-7°	-15°	-23°	-32°	-39°	-46°
40	-1°	-8°	-17°	-26°	-34°	-42°	-50°
48	-2°	-10°	-18°	-27°	-36°	-44°	-58°
56	-2.5°	-11°	-20°	-28°	-37°	-45°	-58°
64	-3°	-12°	-21°	-29°	-39°	-48°	-56°

2. Chart Ryan's data on the graph at the right. Use one line to show the actual temperature and another to show wind chill.

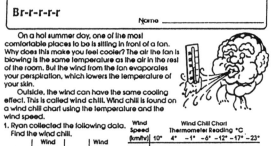

3. Which two days have the same actual temperature?
Monday and Wednesday
Why are the wind chill temperatures different? Stronger wind on Mon.

4. Which day has the largest difference between wind chill and actual temperature?
Saturday

Page 95

Thunderboomers

Name _____

Flash-boom! Two things must happen in order for a thunderstorm to form. First, warm air must rise quickly causing an updraft. Second, the updraft must contain large amounts of water vapor.

As the warm, moist air quickly rises, it cools and condenses into tiny droplets or ice crystals. As a result, a cloud forms. The condensing water vapor warms the air and causes the cloud to build higher and higher, forming a thunderhead.

Each water droplet carries a tiny electrical charge. With each thunderhead containing billions of droplets, the electrical charge builds up. Electricity jumps from the top of the cloud to the bottom causing a giant spark called lightning. The lightning heats the air, causing it to expand rapidly. The rapidly expanding air causes vibrations called thunder.

1. Number the steps in order for the formation of a thunderstorm.

5 a thunderhead forms
1 warm air quickly rises
3 a cloud forms
2 water vapor cools and condenses
4 cloud builds higher and higher

2. Put a ✓ in front of each precaution you should take during a thunderstorm.

✓ remain indoors
___ stand under a tree
✓ stay away from metal fences
___ swim in lakes but not swimming pools
___ carry an umbrella on the golf course
✓ stay away from the television and telephone

Fun Fact
There is enough electricity in one flash of lightning to light your house for a whole year.

Page 96

Answer Key

FLASH-BOOM!

Name _____

FLASH — a bolt of lightning brightens the sky. You slowly count to 15 and then — BOOM — thunder! With this information, you are able to estimate how far the storm is from you.

Lightning and thunder occur at approximately the same time, but you see the lightning before you hear the thunder. That is because light travels much faster than sound. On a typical, warm summer day, sound travels one kilometer in three seconds. How far away is the storm if you count 15 seconds? Follow these steps to find out.

1. Time the FLASH to BOOM in seconds. __15 sec.__

2. Divide the seconds by 3. (3 km/sec)

3. Your answer is in km. __5 km__

$$3\overline{)15} \quad \begin{array}{r} 5 \\ \underline{15} \\ 0 \end{array}$$

(If your answer has a remainder, you may round off to the nearest whole number.)

Matt timed eight FLASH-BOOMS in a storm as it approached and passed. Using Matt's data, find the distance of the storm with each passing FLASH-BOOM. Circle the time and distance when the storm was the closest.

Time	Distance		Time	Distance
1. 63 sec.	21 km	5.	9 sec.	3 km
2. 48 sec.	16 km	6.	3 sec.	1 km
3. 24 sec.	8 km	7.	12 sec.	4 km
4. 18 sec.	6 km	8.	27 sec.	9 km

9. What does it mean if you see a flash and hear a boom at the same time?
The lightning is right next to you.

10. What factors can make our estimation of the distance of the lightning less accurate? Wind speed and direction; air temperature.

Fun Fact
A beam of light travels from the moon to the earth in less than two seconds. It takes almost two weeks for sound to travel the same distance.

Whirlpools of Wind

Name _____

The spinning winds of a twisting funnel cloud, called a tornado, are the most violent winds on Earth. These winds can be as strong as 500 km/hr and travel in a path a few hundred meters wide. Air pressure is so low in the center of the tornado that objects which are in the funnel's path, like houses, explode from the expanding air trapped inside.

No one knows exactly what causes tornadoes. One theory is that a front of moving, cool, dry air overruns warm, moist air. The warm, moist air is trapped below and rushes upwards. More warm air rushes in from the sides and causes warm updrafts to twist and spin. Tornadoes last only a short time, but if they touch the ground they can cause horrible destruction.

To keep us safe during a tornado, the National Weather Bureau issues tornado warnings and tornado watches.

1. What is a tornado watch? Weather conditions are right for a tornado.

2. What is a tornado warning? A tornado has been spotted.

3. What should you do if you are at home when a tornado warning is issued?
_____ Answers will vary. _____

at school? _____

walking in your neighborhood? _____

Solve these tornado twisters.

1. Tornadoes are called **funnel** clouds.

2. The explanation of a tornado's origin is only a **theory**.

3. The **air pressure** in the center of a tornado is very low.

4. Objects **explode** in a tornado.

Fun Fact
In 1973, a tornado in France crossed a pond, sucking everything into the air. A few miles away, there was a surprise "rainfall" of water, fish, and frogs as the tornado dropped its load.

Willy-Willies

Name _____

Over warm oceans in areas near the equator, the world's most powerful storms are formed. These large, rotating masses of warm, moist air, called hurricanes, bring heavy rains and very strong winds.

Hurricanes form when cool, light winds aloft combine with the warm, moist ocean air. This warm, moist air spirals upwards, releasing heat and causing the winds to grow stronger. The winds can reach a speed of 350 km/h and measure over 650 km wide. The eye, or center of the hurricane, may be very calm. Hurricanes move slowly and last for a number of days. The high winds and heavy rains of a hurricane can cause great damage.

Hurricanes are called Willy-Willies in Australia, typhoons in the North Atlantic, cyclones in the Indian Ocean, and Baguios in the Philippine Sea.

Use the information from this page and other sources to compare the characteristics of tornadoes and hurricanes. Place an X in the correct column.

	Tornado	Hurricane
1. Causes much damage to property.	X	X
2. Has very high winds.	X	X
3. Travels a path that is less than a mile wide.	X	
4. Associated with storms near the equator.		X
5. Warnings give as much as two days' notice.		X
6. Given "names" by the National Weather Service.		X
7. Very calm in the center.		X
8. Low air pressure causes objects to explode in its center.	X	
9. Lasts only a few minutes.	X	
10. Causes high ocean tides and waves.		X

Find Out
Hurricanes are given names. How does the National Weather Service decide on the name? What are the names of some of the most destructive hurricanes in the past 30 years?

Mapping the Weather

Name _____

Weather maps show the recorded weather conditions over a large area. These maps are usually made by the computers of the National Weather Service. They are used to help predict weather changes.

There are many types of weather maps. The one on this page is typical of those found in many newspapers. It gives air pressure in units called millibars, written at the end of each isobar.

1. What is the temperature in Seattle? 8°

2. What is the direction of the wind in Miami? East

3. What city has fog? Atlanta

4. What kind of front is east of Oklahoma City? Cold

5. What kind of front is north of Atlanta? Warm

6. What kind of front was formed where the cold front met the warm front? Occluded

7. What kind of cloud cover is found in Miami? Clear

8. What is the cloud cover like in Boston? Partly cloudy

9. What is the barometric pressure in millibars for the city of Seattle? 1014

Something Special
If you would like accurate weather maps of your own, contact the meteorologists at the nearest large radio or T.V. station.

Answer Key

"Red Sky at Night"

Name _____

"Will Saturday be a good day to go the beach?" Better look at the weather forecast. The National Weather Service makes short range forecasts (up to three days) using basic weather instruments, information from weather maps, and records of past weather patterns. Use the information from the chart to make weather predictions for the situations below.

Wind Direction	Sea-Level Barometric Pressure (mm)	Weather to be Expected
SW to NW	764.54 to 767.08, steady	Fair, with little temperature change for 1-2 days.
SW to NW	764.58 to 767.08, rising fast	Fair, followed by rain within 2 days.
SW to NW	767.08 and above, steady	Continued fair, no marked temperature change.
S to E	756.92 or below, falling fast	Severe storm, followed within 24 hours by clearing and, in winter, colder temperatures.
S to SW	762.00 or below, rising slowly	Clearing within a few hours, fair for several days.
Going to W	745.00 or below, rising fast	Clearing and colder.
E to N	756.92 or below, falling fast	Severe NE gale and heavy rain. In winter, heavy snow and cold wave.
SE to NE	762.00 or below, falling slowly	Steady rain for 1-2 days.
SE to NE	762.00 or below, falling fast	Rain, high wind, clearing in 36 hours and cooler.
S to SE	764.58 to 767.08, falling slowly	Rain within 24 hours.

Data

1. Southwest wind, barometric pressure 767.20mm, steady _Cont. fair, no marked temp. change._

2. South wind, barometric pressure 765.00, falling slowly _Rain within 24 hours._

3. South wind, barometric pressure 756.00, falling fast _Severe storm, followed w/in 24 hrs. by clearing._

4. Southeast wind, barometric pressure 761.51, falling slowly _Steady rain for 1-2 days._

5. Southwest wind, barometric pressure 765.10, steady _Fair, little temp. change for 1-2 days._

6. What kind of weather usually comes with rising barometric pressure? _Fair_

7. What kind of weather usually comes with falling barometric pressure? _Stormy_

Find Out

Weather Proverbs: Ask your parents about weather proverbs in your area, such as, "Red sky at night, sailors delight. Red sky in morn', sailors forewarn."

Page 101

Weather Tools

Name _____

Meteorologists use many basic instruments to gather their data. You may already have many of these instruments in your home. If not, you can construct them from easy-to-find materials. Many fine books are available that show you how to construct your own weather station.

Modern forecasting also relies on many sophisticated electronic instruments. Radar is used to track areas of precipitation hundreds of miles away. Pictures of cloud formations from all over the world are available from weather-tracking satellites.

Solve the puzzle using both the picture clues and the written clues.

Down
1. Cloud direction indicator.
2. Precipitation is measured with a rain _____.
3. Measures air pressure.
4. A weather _____ shows wind direction.

Across
5. Measures relative humidity.
6. Measures wind speed.
7. Measures temperature.

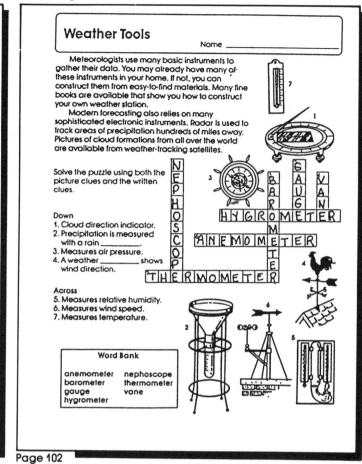

Word Bank	
anemometer	nephoscope
barometer	thermometer
gauge	vane
hygrometer	

Crossword answers: NEPHOSCOPE, BAROMETER, GAUGE, VANE, HYGROMETER, ANEMOMETER, THERMOMETER

Page 102

About the book . . .

This book will enhance your science program with entertaining, interesting and informative activities covering such diverse topics as the human body, plants, astronomy, weather, earth science, and the animal kingdom.

About the author . . .

Daryl Vriesenga holds a Master's Degree from Michigan State University in Science Education. He has taught at the elementary level for over eighteen years. He is the author of several science books for the elementary classroom, including **Science Fair Projects**, **Science Activities**, **Earth Science** and **The Human Body**, among others.

Credits . . .

Author: Daryl Vriesenga
Editor: Jackie Servis
Artists: Sandra W. Ludwig and Dan Cool
Production: Pat Geasler and Mike Denhof
Cover Photo: Dan Van Duinen